Tenerife

Text and design by Roger Williams
Principal photographer: Mike Griffiths
Picture Editor: Hilary Genin
Managing Editor: Tony Halliday

Berlitz POCKET GUIDE

Tenerife

First Edition 2004
Updated 2005

PHOTOGRAPHY

Berlitz 20, 42; Chris Coe 40, 43, 45, 61, 62, 80, 88; Andrew Eames 19; Mike Griffiths 1, 3TR, 6, 9, 11, 15, 16, 22, 31, 49, 50, 53, 54, 56, 58, 60, 67, 69, 71, 73, 75, 76, 77, 82, 83, 85, 89, 91, 96, 97, 98, 101, 103; Gary-John Norman 8, 12, 24, 26, 34, 36, 59, 63, 66, 74, 93; Mark Read 78, 79, 94; Roger Williams 17, 28, 29, 32, 33, 37, 39, 44, 46, 48, 64, 65, 70, 87, 100
Cover picture: Robert Harding Picture Library

CONTACTING THE EDITORS

Every effort has been made to provide accurate information in this publication, but changes are inevitable. The publisher cannot be responsible for any resulting loss, inconvenience or injury. We would appreciate it if readers would call our attention to any errors or outdated information by contacting Berlitz Publishing, PO Box 7910, London SE1 1WE, England.
Fax: (44) 20 7403 0290;
e-mail: berlitz@apaguide.co.uk
www.berlitzpublishing.com

© 2005 Apa Publications GmbH & Co. Verlag KG, Singapore Branch, Singapore

Printed in Singapore by Insight Print Services (Pte) Ltd, 38 Joo Koon Road, Singapore 628990.
Tel: (65) 6865-1600. Fax: (65) 6861-6438

Berlitz Trademark Reg. U.S. Patent Office and other countries. Marca Registrada

Playa de las Teresitas (page 32), the main beach for Santa Cruz and the only yellow sand outside the main resorts

Casa de los Balcones (page 46) in La Orotava is th best example o traditional tow mansion

El Teide (page 5. Spain's highe mounta

TOP TEN ATTRACTIONS

seo de la
uraleza y
l Hombre
ge 29) in
ta Cruz is
e largest
museum
▼

Jardín Botánico (page 44) in Puerto de la Cruz, used as a staging post for New World flora, is full of exotic plants

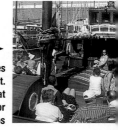

The harbour at Los Gigantes (page 67) on the west coast. Situated beneath sheer cliffs that give it its name, the resort is a major centre for diving and boat trips

San Cristóbal de la Laguna (page 34), the island's former capital, is a UNESCO World Heritage Site ▼

Masca (page 65) is a beautiful, remote village with a track to the sea

Castillo de
Miguel in
Garachico
e 62), the
rmer port

➤

Parque Etnográfico Pirámides de Güímar (page 77), founded by the explorer Thor Heyerdahl ➤

CONTENTS

Fact Sheets

INTRODUCTION

Time signals on state radio and television in Spain give two times: one for mainland Spain and one for 'Las Canarias'. Adrift in the Atlantic Ocean more than 1,000km (620 miles) to the south, and 115km (70 miles) from the west coast of Africa, Tenerife and the 12 other islands that make up the Canary archipelago don't see the sun rise until around one hour later than their mainland compatriots.

At just over 2,000 sq km (around 800 sq miles), Tenerife is the largest of these volcanic cones that began to erupt from the depths of the Atlantic bed 20 million years ago. Six are tiny and uninhabited. Of the others, the three closest to Africa (Gran Canaria, Lanzarote and Fuertaventura) are geologically the oldest, formed 10 million years before Tenerife. Finally, some 2 million years after that, the Canary's other western isles of La Palma, La Gomera and El Hierro burst into life.

The nearest island to Tenerife is La Gomera 30km (18 miles) west. Gran Canaria, capital of the eastern isles, is 60km (36 miles) southwest, and the sea between them is 2,000m (6,560ft) deep.

Volcanic Landscape

On a clear day all the islands can be seen from the top of Tenerife's Pico del Teide, at 3,718m (12,195ft) the highest mountain in the whole of Spain. Its peak was formed a million years ago inside the crater of a former, collapsed volcano, the Circo de Cañadas, where the landscape is burnt and hauntingly bleak. There has been no volcanic activity

The road to Masca

Formations at Cumbre Dorsal

here for 500,000 years, though eruptions have occurred elsewhere on the island, the last in 1909 on Montaña Chinyero, near Santiago del Tiede. Lava fields created by the volcanoes are only part of a diversity of landscapes on an island the shape of an inverted triangle of just 2,034 sq km (785 sq miles). It includes tropical gardens, misty forests, fertile mountain slopes, tranquil villages, rocky headlands and black beaches, the most popular of which have been lined with imported Sahara sand.

Climate

The climate on Tenerife is pleasant all year round, with little variation in the average annual temperature of around 22°C (72°F). It is this attractive climate that has made the Canaries such a popular holiday destination. The Teide massif effectively divides Tenerife into two climatic zones, north and south. The northerly trade winds result in more cloud cover and rainfall in the north, with the coast enjoying a constant, warm, subtropical climate. Cloud conditions constantly vary, making it sometimes hard to know exactly what to expect. Higher up, in the cloud layer between 500 and 1,200m (1,600–4,000ft), it is cooler and more humid and the sun generally shines only in the mornings. Above the cloud layer the temperatures vary greatly between day and night; in winter they drop below freezing and snow falls, creating small lakes as it melts. The south of the island, where the popular tourist beaches have sprung up, is hot and dry, reaching almost desert conditions. Clouds are rare and there is little rainfall, but the sirocco wind from the south occasionally causes a sandy haze called the *calima*. A steady wind on the south coast creates ideal windsurfing conditions.

Flora and Fauna

These climatic conditions and the unusual geological features have nurtured a variety of plants and wildlife, some of which are unique to the island. Comparable with Hawaii, the Galapagos and other archipelagos that have their own biodiversity, the Canary Islands as a whole have around 650 native species and nearly 40 percent of the territory is under some sort of conservation. On Tenerife 400 of the 2,000 naturally-occurring plant species are endemic.

Bird of paradise, the Canaries' adopted flower and a major export

The extraordinary environment has attracted botanists down the centuries. From Germany came Alexander von Humboldt, who, in the 19th century, stopped on his way to South America and gave the islands fulsome praise. The French diplomat Sabin Berthelot, an enthusiast for all things Canarian, arrived on the island in 1820 at the age of 26 and became director of the botanical gardens. From England in 1875 came Marianne North, whose works fill the gallery named after her at Kew Gardens in London.

What they found were tree-sized poinsettias, local variants of laurel and euphorbia, the *Phoenix canariensis* palm and the legendary dragon tree *(Dracaena draco)*. Among many flowers that make the island particularly attractive in May and June are red pillars of Teide echium or 'pride of Tenerife' *(orgullo di Tenerife)* and the pink-and-white Teide broom *(Spartocytisus nubigens)*, both of which thrive in the arid Cañadas.

The island has several thousand species of insects, though none is likely to do you any harm. There are grasshoppers native to each island, and the ones on Tenerife grow to 12cm (5in). Its resident reptiles include the Canary species of lizard, skink and gecko.

Bird Life

Many of the birds found on Tenerife will be familiar to Europeans, but there are different ones to look out for, too. Most are shy, however, and stay out of the sun, and though a variety of coloured doves are evident, don't expect to see many species as you travel around. The blue Teide finch, for example, might be seen in the National Park. Forests of Canarian pines are home to the blue chaffinch and the canary, a dull bird in the wild, which becomes yellow and more boisterous when caged (or blinded, as they once were to make them sing louder). In the scrubland you might see the Canarian pipit, Barbary partridge or Trumpeter finch. In the laurel and juniper forests look out for the Canary Island kinglet and native pigeons. Other unusual species include the collared pratincole, American golden plover, glossy ibis and Barbary falcon.

You will see ocean birds around the headlands or if you go whale- or dolphin-watching. The Canaries are on one of the principal migration routes for whales: one third of all species pass through Canarian waters each year. *(For details of bird-watching, see page 84.)*

Ecology

The island's habitat is continually under pressure, particularly from the four million tourists who arrive each year, making heavy demands on local resources. Tree felling, which began after the European conquest, has divested the island of lakes and rivers, and water is a precious commodity. Visitors should not be profligate with it. In addition water treatment means that the taste might not always be great, so buying bottled water is both ecologically defensible and practical here.

Ecology is on every islander's mind, as new cement-block villas and apartments continue to spread over the landscape. Summer forest fires, too, have disastrous effects, often started by careless

Harnessing the trade winds

tourists. Environmental protection groups are active in a place where nature is the driving cultural force.

Population

The resident population, including some 25,000 expatriates, is around 700,000, more than half living in the conurbation of Santa Cruz. In the southern resorts where most visitors go, you are likely to encounter *godos* from Gallicia and other poorer regions of the Spanish mainland, who come here to find work. *Tinerfeños* are cheerful, gregarious and courteous, with a love of children, parties and football. According to a folk song, 'Canarians are like the giant

Tinerfeña in a straw hat

Teide, quiet as snow on the outside and fire in the heart'. Their carnival is, after all, one of the greatest in the world. No trace of the tall, fair-haired Guanche survives, though recent DNA sampling, using Guanche (*see page 14*) mummies, shows traces in a percentage of islanders.

The local Spanish accent is halfway between Madrid and Mexico. The 'c' and 'z' are not a lisped *th* as they are on the mainland, and consonants at the end of words sometimes fall away (Santa Cru', La' Palma', for instance, and Juá instead of Juan). Some words have come directly from South

America (*gwa-gwa* for a bus), others from their colonial past – *chóni* for a foreigner, from the English 'Johnny' foreigner.

Economy

Tourism is the main occupation of the islanders today. Agriculture is on the wane and some of the more remote villages have become abandoned. Since the conquest the island has had a series of monocultures, from sugar to bananas and cochineal. Bananas are still one of the main crops, along with tomatoes and cut flowers, particularly the bird of paradise flower *(strelitzia)*. Wine making is limited to domestic consumption.

> The native island dog is the Verdino. Smooth-haired and powerful, it weighs 40–50kg (90–110lb) and gets its name from its slightly greenish colour. There is a theory that the islands were named after the native dogs (*canes* in Latin) found here in classical times.

There are no mineral resources on the island, and no industry. Its ports have suffered with the decades-long shipping decline. Because produce and manufactured goods have to be shipped in, the cost of living tends to be higher than in mainland Spain.

Government

The Canary Islands are one of the autonomous regions of Spain and a member of the European Union. Santa Cruz de Tenerife is the administrative capital of the western islands and Las Palmas on Gran Canario the capital of the eastern islands. The presidency, which coincides with local elections, rotates between the two capitals every four years. The 60-member parliament meets in the parliament building in Santa Cruz, while the Supreme Court sits in Las Palmas.

A BRIEF HISTORY

La Orotava Valley behind Puerto de la Cruz on the north coast of Tenerife is the most fertile and pleasant on the island. When the Hispanic conquerors arrived in the 15th century they found the Taora living here, the richest of nine island tribes, whose chief or *mencey* was called Tanasú. These tall, fair-skinned, blue-eyed people called Guanches somehow reached the Canary Islands in the 1st or 2nd century BC from northwest Africa, and were related to Berbers. They developed a written language, which remains largely undeciphered, and were ruled through councils called *tagorors*, with their court in Adeje on the west coast.

The island provided natural shelter with many caves (in Chinameda and Fasnia caves are still used today), which they decorated, and they built stone huts, too.

Guanche Culture

Not surprisingly, the volcanic giant of El Teide was central to worship for the Guanches. Their culture can be glimpsed through their funerary rites and in particular their mummifying rituals, which are explained at the Museo de la Naturaleza y el Hombre in Santa Cruz. They probably worshipped the sun, and the ancient 'pyramids' that the Norwegian explorer Thor Heyerdahl revealed in 1990 in Güímar are convincing evidence of how their ritual buildings may have looked.

The Guanches built no boats, nor did the wheel occur to them, but they were

> The Guanches are supposedly related to Berbers, but how they reached the Canary Islands from Africa is a mystery. The Romans arrived to find that the islanders did not possess boats.

Guanche community, from Pueblochico near Puerto de la Cruz

adept potters, making their finest vessels for religious purposes and storing grain. Pottery and cultivation was women's work. Men hunted and tended the animals. A lack of metal ore on the island left the Guanches stuck in the stone age, with blunt instruments sharpened by bones and black volcanic obsidian, found in the Cañadas.

For food they hunted wild cats and pigs, Barbary partridges and quail. They also kept pigs, sheep and, principally, goats, whose skins were the material of the 'loose cassocks' that they wore. But it was as a land of dogs that the island group may have been given its name. In the 1st century AD Pliny wrote of an expedition to the islands by King Juba II of Mauretania, who apparently saw many dogs roaming there. *Canis* is the Latin for dog, hence Canary Islands. The islands were fixed on the earliest classical maps as the *'Insulae Fortunatae'*, the Fortunate Islands, and were the furthest western point of the known world.

The Conquest

Spanish cartographers properly mapped the islands at the end of the 14th century when the name Tenerife (actually 'Tenerifiz') appeared for the first time. The Genoese Lanzarotto Malocello is generally thought to have led the first European expedition to the Canaries, landing in the 1330s on the island that bears his name. Within a few decades conquest of the islands began. Jean de Béthencourt, a Norman adventurer employed by Henri III of Castile, made the initial advances, capturing the eastern isles and then, in 1405, El Hierro, smallest of the western isles. Tenerife, the most populous of the islands, was still in Guanche hands in 1492 when Christopher Columbus stopped at neighbouring Gran Canaria and La Gomera on his way to the New World (noting, as he did so, an eruption of El Teide, and recording that his crew thought it a sign that they should turn back).

Missionary's Betrayal

That same year, Alfonso Fernandez de Lugo, a mercenary backed by Genoese merchants, seized La Palma, following a six-year campaign against Gran Canaria. Only Tenerife remained in native hands.

Guanche cult of the dead

The influence of the conquerors of the other islands had spread to Tenerife and de Lugo's way was paved by the missionary activities of a native woman convert and lay preacher, Francisca de Gazmira. On the coast de Lugo easily defeated local tribes, moving to the better defended interior where he tricked chief Tanasú of the

Taoro tribe with a sham parley. Finally, however, he was caught in a trap at Barranco de Acentejo (now the town of La Matanza, the slaughter) 16km (10 miles) into the Orotava Valley.

De Lugo escaped to return to the island with a larger force the following year and win a decisive victory on the plains of La Vitoria de Acentejo, a couple of miles south of his earlier defeat. Some 2,000 Guanches were cut down by the sophisticated Spanish crossbow, and Tanasú, the last chief of the Taoro, committed suicide.

De Lugo established his capital at San Cristóbal de la

Guanche chief

Laguna in the middle of the fertile Valle de Aguerre, in striking distance of both the north and east coasts. Here the statue of Jesus that he had brought to the island came to rest in the Santuario del Cristo, and the flag that had claimed Tenerife for Spain was subsequently hung in the town hall. Santa Iglesia cathedral, which was founded ten years later in 1515, became de Lugo's resting place.

The effect of the conquerors on the local population was disastrous. The new diseases they brought spread among the Guanche population and many were taken into slavery, though the nobles were accorded due respect, and some of them intermarried. From the thousands that had inhabited the island, soon only a few hundred remained. The investors in de Lugo's expedition were rewarded with lucrative plots of land in the west, where sugar cane was introduced and refineries built at Realejos, Duate and Icod. To fuel the new economy de Lugo continued to seek Italian finance, and Portuguese workers were imported to harvest the canes on a share-cropping basis.

Sugar and Wine

The landscape began to change, too. Mills were stoked with timber cut from the forests, which had the long-term effect of reducing rainfall and drying up lakes, streams and springs.

Canarian sugar could not compete with that being planted in the New World, and by the end of the 15th century vineyards of the Malvasía grape had been established on the east of the island, and it was wine that offered an alternative economy as the sugar trade slumped. The grape produced sweet, dessert wines that travelled well and was particularly enjoyed by northern Europeans. By the time Shakespeare's Falstaff and Sir Toby Belch were downing 'cups of Canary', and Bostonians were talking of 'the Isles of Wine', it had become the major export.

The Canary Islands benefited from being on the trade route to the New World, and ships regularly blew in and out of Tenerife's excellent harbours, principally Garachico on the north coast, carrying sugar and slaves. Trade between Spain and the New World was confined to Spanish nationals, so smuggling and piracy became part of daily life. But in 1610 the Spanish government relaxed this restriction and a new aristocracy bub-

As they died out, Guanches were romanticised in literature as 'noble savages'. The Spanish dramatist Félix Lope de Vega (1562–1635) created for them an idyll a long way from reality.

San Cristóbal de la Laguna, the island's first capital

bled up as foreign capitalists headed for Tenerife. By the mid-century the island had 1,500 English and Dutch residents out of a population of 50,000.

The Rise of Puerto de la Cruz

Malvasía's rival was Madeira, from the Portuguese island of the same name, and when England sided with Portugal in the War of the Spanish Succession (1701–14) a major market was lost. But for another century Tenerife continued to be the islands' major wine producer, and the wealth that it brought paid for the rich architecture of the wine towns such as Orotava. In 1706, when a volcanic eruption devastated Garachico, Puerto de la Cruz (then Puerto de la Orotava) became the island's principal port.

A university was founded in La Laguna at the start of the 18th century and an intelligentsia flourished among the 70,000 *tinerfeños*. But prosperity did not survive the century and the wine trade diminished. Global conflict, with both America's War of Independence and the Napoleonic wars, during which Admiral Nelson blockaded Santa Cruz, was harmful to trade. Hardship was compounded by revolutions in Latin America, where many Canarians had gone to seek their fortunes, and payments to the families left behind were disrupted. The Canaries were themselves not without revolutionary fervour, and in 1819 the local junta put forward the islanders' desire to 'get rid of all the Spaniards now here and to put the people of this land in their place'.

Beetles to Bananas

After trade in wine had slumped, the cochineal beetle was introduced from Mexico, mainly in the eastern isles. This had a brutalising effect on the landscape as native trees were replaced by cactus for the beetle to feed on. The crop went

Banana workers, 1920

into decline when synthetic dyes were introduced in the late 19th century, by which time bananas, said to have been introduced by the French consul, Sabin Berthelot, were making money.

In 1822 Santa Cruz had become the official capital of the archipelago and 30 years later each island was granted free trade status for one of its ports, though Tenerife had two: Puerto de la Cruz and Santa Cruz, which then had the archipelago's only first-class road, to La Orotava.

Secindino Delgado was the most influential independence figure. He went to work in Cuba at 14, but it was in Venezuela, in 1897, that he founded *El Guanche*, a newspaper calling for independence in the Canary Islands.

Tenerife's superiority took a knock in 1881 when a harbour improvement scheme for Las Palmas on Gran Canaria led to the eclipse of Santa Cruz. When refrigeration arrived at the end of the 19th century, tourists came, too, travelling on the fruit boats. To cater for them the Grand Hotel Taoro in Puerto de la Cruz was built in 1892, and for many years it was the largest hotel in Spain.

The Civil War

The Spanish Second Republic of 1931 brought new hopes of autonomy but General Franco's uprising of 1936 put paid to any such aspirations for more than 40 years. Well-known for his right-wing sentiments and suspected of plans against the Republican government, Franco had been sent to Tenerife in March to put him out of harm's way. From here, however, he flew from Las Palmas to the Spanish North African enclave of Melilla on 18 July. Two days later the uprising that led to the three-year civil war was under way and the islands were in Franco's hands – La Palma took a hefty shelling from the navy before being overcome. On Tenerife, Lt Gonzales

**Tourism, the new
monoculture**

Campos was the only officer to oppose the uprising and he was shot, along with the civil governor. Republican prisoners and suspects were herded into Fyffes' banana warehouse, near Santa Cruz football ground, and shot in batches. Friend of Hitler and Mussolini, Franco was ostracised by the rest of the world until the early 1950s when Spain was welcomed back into the international community in exchange for accepting Nato bases.

Tourism and the Post-Franco Years

After direct flights to Tenerife started in 1959, tourism began with a vengeance. Pressure on Puerto de la Cruz to build ever more hotels caused people within the area to sell up and transfer their plantations to the south, piping water into a region that had hitherto been dry, and opening up the barren lands in Adeje and Arona. On this coast, tourists in search of a tan flocked to the port of Los Cristianos. And this is where the boom really happened, sprawling up into Playa de las Américas, which was created in 1978, the same year that the nearby airport of Reina Sofía opened.

Queen Sofía, after whom the airport is named, is the wife of King Juan Carlos, who returned to the Spanish throne and restored democracy after Franco's death in 1975. Three years later a new Constitution granted degrees of autonomy to Spain's regions, including the Canary Islands. As in other parts of Spain, all but the fiercely separatist were appeased.

Historical Landmarks

circa 3000BC settlers arrive from Africa.

206BC Guanches reach the island.

1st century AD Classical writers describe the islands on the edge of the known world populated by dogs (*canis*, hence Canaries).

1st–13th centuries Guanche society develops under tribal chiefs.

1440s Jean de Béthencourt, a Norman adventurer, captures the island of Hierro but fails to take Tenerife.

1492 Christopher Columbus witnesses eruption of Mt Teide en route to discovering the Americas.

1495 Tanasú, the last chief of the Taoro, commits suicide when Tenerife is conquered by Alfonso Fernandez de Lugo at the Battle of Acentejo. De Lugo introduces sugar mills.

17th century Wine replaces sugar as the main product.

1656 Sixteen Spanish galleons bringing gold from the Americas are sunk in Santa Cruz harbour by the British under Admiral Blake.

1701–14 The Canaries' university founded in La Laguna.

1706 Mt Teide erupts, destroying the main port of Garachico.

1797 Admiral Nelson's attack on Santa Cruz repelled.

1810 The first appeals for independence from Madrid.

1822 Santa Cruz becomes the capital of the archipelago, which is made a free trade zone.

1850–1900 Large scale emigration to Latin America.

1880s Bananas introduced.

1892 Grand Hotel Taoro, the largest in Spain, built in Puerto de la Cruz.

1927 The Canaries are divided into two provinces, with Santa Cruz administering the four western islands.

1936 General Franco launches his rebellion from Tenerife at the start of the three-year Spanish Civil War.

1959 First direct flights to Tenerife bring a new wave of tourists.

1978 The Canaries become autonomous within Spain.

1995 Spain becomes a full member of the European Union.

2002 The euro replaces the peseta as the currency of Spain.

GETTING AROUND

Because the island is not large, it is easy to make forays from any base. Nowhere is far away, as cruise-ships passengers discover when, docking in Santa Cruz with just four hours ashore, they find they have enough time for a coach to take them to the top of El Teide and back, stopping off at La Orotava for some souvenirs, or even to hire a car and make their own way up to the cable car at the summit.

For much of the island you don't need a car. Buses are regular and inexpensive. From the capital, Santa Cruz, you can have a day out on the opposite coast in Puerto de la Cruz, the popular north coast resort, stopping off at the UNESCO World Heritage site of La Laguna, with enough time to enjoy both places at leisure and return later in the day. From Los Cristianos and Playa de las Américas in the south, you can have a day out in these places, too. A hire car of course adds convenience and allows you to stop to photograph a view (they are always spectacular) or to inspect the flowers, or to take advantage of signs of honey or wine for sale.

The descriptions that follow start in Santa Cruz, and continue anti-clockwise around the island.

THE NORTHEAST

Santa Cruz de Tenerife
Tenerife's capital and principal port is on the northeastern arm of the island, facing south and looking towards Gran Canaria, its rival, an hour's jet-foil ferry trip away. The city

Playa de las Teresitas, with Santa Cruz in the distance

The Plaza de España, hub of Santa Cruz

doesn't have a real heart, a municipal or cathedral square, but the main action takes place on the pedestrianised streets and squares leading up from the port and also on the Rambla that sweeps round the top of the town.

The extensive waterfront of docks and quays comes to climax at **Plaza de España**: to the west are the container ports and the industrial part of town, to the east the jacaranda-lined Avenida de Anaga passes beside the ferry port and yachting harbour. The Plaza de España is the focus of rallies and fiestas, when the streets are sealed off around the central **Monumento de los Caídos**, a monument to the fallen Nationalists in the Civil War watched over by a couple of Guanche chiefs. The distinctive art deco building beside it, with a clock tower, is the **Cabildo Insular**, with offices of the island's *cabildo*, or government, and the post office headquarters. To the left of the entrance is the main tourist office for Santa Cruz and the island.

Shopping Area

Running up from the Plaza España is **Plaza Candelaria**, where a statue of the island's patron dates from 1772. This is the start of the main pedestrianised shopping area and the pavement cafés are a popular meeting place. **Calle del Castillo**, the principal shopping street, heads inland past the **Parlamento de Canarias**, on the right. The original 1898 neoclassical building, designed by Antonio Pintor, has been augmented to include the buildings fronting Castillo, with a green metal construction on its upper floors. Calle del Castillo ends at **Plaza del General Weyler**, a place of war and peace, where the Fuente de Amor (Fountain of Love) by the Genoese Achille Caresse is overlooked by the Capitania General, the islands' military headquarters where Franco was stationed when he started the Civil War.

On the north side of Calle del Castillo is the **Plaza del Principe de Asturias**, one of the town's most pleasant squares. El Principio café and restaurant, in a turn-of-the-20th-century iron-and-glass building, is an excellent place to stop for a coffee or *tapas*. On the south side of the square, beside the bright art nouveau Circulo de Amistad, is the **Museo Municipal de Bellas Artes** (open Tues–Fri 10am–8pm, Sat–Sun 10am–2pm; free). The front of the building has busts of poets, philosophers and musicians. Inside is the town library and, on the first and second floors, a gallery of paintings from the 16th to the 20th centuries. These include a panoramic picture of the foundation of Santa Cruz by Alonso de Lugo in 1494, two years after he had taken the island, and among portraits of the local aristocracy

Santa Cruz entered the *Guinness World Records* when a record crowd of a quarter of a million filled the Plaza España for the 1987 carnival. The Tenerife carnival is said to be the second-biggest in the world after Rio.

Nuestra Señora de la Concepción

is one of the romantically windswept French consul and botanist Sabin Berthelot who did so much for the island's plant life.

Behind the museum is the **Iglesia de San Francisco**, founded in 1680 and part of a former convent where concerts sometimes take place.

The Oldest Church

Eight years after Santa Cruz was founded, the very first chapel was built where the city's main church, **Nuestra Señora de la Concepción** stands today, just to the west of the Cabildo Insular. The cross that de Lugo brought ashore is among its treasures. In 1652 the church was rebuilt after a fire, its octagonal tower acting as a look-out point. The lovely balcony on its exterior, a feature of church architecture throughout the island, gives its west front a curiously domestic appearance. Inside, the space is cool and impressive and the beautiful coffered *mudéjar* style ceiling is also typical of the island.

In the streets around the cathedral are some of the oldest buildings in Santa Cruz and they have been attractively maintained in warm earth colours. Stop for a drink in Tapas Antigua opposite the church, or in J.C. Murphy's in the little church square, or join the arty crowd in Tasca El Porrón further up Carrer de Dominguez Alfonso, where local musicians meet.

If you are strolling here in the evening, you may be lucky to chance on street theatre in which performers use the doors and balconies of the houses to put on their entertainments. Nearby is the legitimate theatre, **Teatro Guimerá**, named after the playwright Angel Guimerá, born in Santa Cruz in 1849, and making his name in Barcelona with *Terra Baixa* in 1896. La Recova, the 1851 building next to the theatre, has been housing **El Centro de Fotografia 'Isla de Tenerife'** until its move to the **Instituto Óscar Domínguez de Arte y Cultura Contemporanea**, the nearby cultural centre designed by Tate Modern architects Herzog & de Meuron, opening in 2005.

Across the Barranco

From Nuestra Señora de la Concepción a bridge crosses a *barranco* (dry river bed) to the former town hospital, now the **Museo de la Naturaleza y el Hombre** (open Tues–Sun 9am–7pm; admission fee). As the name implies, all island life is here, and this is a good starting point for understanding Tenerife in all its geographical and historical aspects. Set out on three floors around two courtyards, it swarms with

Círculo de Amistad

schoolchildren in term-time, but is large enough to allow you to browse in peace. The island's flora and fauna are fully explained, as is its geology, with descriptions of winds, currents and volcanoes. Man features early on, with mummified Guanches, and displays show how the indigenous population lived. At the end is a café and an excellent bookshop.

Behind the museum, off Calle San Sebastián, is the **Mercado de Nuestra Señora de Africa**. A morning market, on two floors, shows the bounty of the island piled high, full of flowers and aromatic herbs. On Sundays there is a flea market, and stalls extend down Calle José Manuel Guimerá.

Latest Developments

Calle José Manuel Guimerá leads down to the main highway, Avenida del Tres de Mayo, which connects the docks to the Autopista del Norte, while the Avenida de la Constitución continues past the port towards the Autopista del Sur. The latter has become the focus of post-millennium developments with an elegant new **Auditorio**, a concert hall designed by the Basque architect Santiago Calatrava, which is home to the Tenerife Symphony Orchestra and the place to see opera and dance. Beside it is a new bus station, and behind it, be-

---

Gentlemen at War

In 1797 Admiral Nelson attacked Santa Cruz. Leading the night assault, he leapt ashore only to have his right elbow shattered by grapeshot from a cannon in the Castillo de Paso Alto. The assault was a failure but the Spanish Governor sent each captured man back to his ship with a bottle of wine and a loaf of bread. His arm amputated, Nelson returned the compliment by sending the governor cheese and a cask of beer. The captured British flags, are stored in a glass case in Nuestra Señora de le Concepción.

The Auditorio, home of the Tenerife Symphony Orchestra

yond the old **Castillo San Juan**, is the **Parque Marítimo César Manrique** (open daily 9am–5pm; admission fee), a breezy area of azur sea-water pools in imitation of the area in Puerto de la Cruz designed by the Lanzarote artist César Manrique, with trees, flowers and waterfalls. With a cafeteria and restaurant, a day out here is as good as on the beach. Beside it is a **Palmetum** with palm trees from all over the world.

The Rambla

Santa Cruz's other main avenue, the **Rambla**, meanders around the back of the town and arrives at the Avenida de Anaga, by the waterfront beside a brutal modernist memorial next to the **Museo Militar Regional de Canarias** (open Tues–Sun 10am–2pm; free). This contains some of the armour worn by the Spanish conquerors, souvenirs from Nelson's attack, including El Tigre, the cannon that shattered his right elbow *(see opposite)*, and the background to Franco's uprising in 1936. The Rambla's central pedestrian walkway, under jacaranda and Judas trees, makes it ideal for the evening *passeo* (stroll). Outdoor sculpture exhibitions have been held here since the 1970s and Henry Moore's *Goslar Warrior* is among a number of works that remain. To add to the pleasures of the Rambla, there are Chinese, Lebanese and Italian restaurants, the old Cine Victor and the bull ring, used mainly for pop concerts. The Rambla also passes the town's largest park, the 6-hectare (15-acre) **Parque García Sanabria**, which has exotic plants and a pleasant café.

The City's Beach

Avenida de Anaga continues north, following the coast past the yacht clubs from where the tycoon Robert Maxwell set sail for the last time in 1991, then towards the town's playground, **Playa de las Teresitas** (served by the No. 10 bus).

Playa de la Teresitas

Stretching 1.5km (1 mile), it's the most golden beach on the island, its imported Sahara sand lapped by shallow waters: dogs, surfboards, ball games and the hanging of towels or clothes on trees are all banned. Kiosks sell snacks, and at weekends locals enliven the atmosphere in the restaurants, notably the Confredí de Pescadores by the fishermen's shacks. There are more places to eat in **San Andrés**, the fish-

Picturesque Igueste

ing village of the original port, where the road heads into the Anaga Hills. After 15 minutes' drive the road reaches the **Mirador de Rozasosa**, offering a last, stunning glimpse of the coast as well as walks through the glorious, herb-scented hills.

On the coast beyond Playa de las Teresitas the road winds without let-up, with the exception of the **Punta de los Organos** *mirador*, which provides a last chance to look down on the beach. A couple of kilometres further on, a turn leads down to the secluded beach of Las Gaviotas beneath the cliffs, where swimsuits are an option. The road ends at **Igueste**, an attractive cluster of white villas among terraces of mangoes and avocados, winding steeply down before coming to a stop several hundred metres short of a small grey beach. From here you can walk to the little beach and one-family hamlet of **Antequera**. The Rincon de Anaga is a popular little family-run restaurant at the entrance to Igueste.

La Laguna

In 1999 **San Cristóbal de la Laguna** became a UNESCO World Heritage Site. Designated the capital of Tenerife by the island's conqueror, Alonso de Lugo, it is visibly the most ancient town on the island, with mansions dating from the 15th century. It is generally known simply as La Laguna, but the lagoon on which it was once sited and named after has long disappeared. The town remains the centre of a large agricultural district, and a cradle of learning and religion, with a university and bishop's see.

Just inland from Santa Cruz, La Laguna is regarded as a suburb of the capital, but in the 20 minutes or so that it takes to reach it, the climate can noticeably cool, and you should be prepared with warmer clothing. The pleasure in being in La Laguna is in simply wandering around its level streets; the lack of inclines is particularly welcome. The old part of town,

Intricately carved balcony, La Laguna

the *casco histórico*, is on a grid system, and the starting point of a visit should be the **Plaza del Adelantado**, where maps of the main sites are distributed from a quaint tourist office booth. The market at the back of the square, piled high with all sorts of fruit and vegetables, as well as caged birds and puppies, is particularly popular on Saturdays and Sundays, when parking is difficult and the square's bars are buzzing. On the opposite side of the square are a trio of impressive but disparate buildings. To the left is the neoclassical **Ayuntamiento** (town hall), which contains the flag that de Lugo planted when he arrived from Spain. To the right is the **Palacio de Nava**, a baroque mansion that belonged, in the early 18th century, to the Marquis de Villanueva de Prado, whose glittering salon attracted the thinkers of the day. He was also responsible for establishing the Botanic Garden in La Orotava. In between is the massive **Iglesia-Convento de Santa Catalina de Siena**, with a 'Canarian' balcony on the corner from where the nuns can glimpse the outside world.

Carrer Obispo Rei Redondo leads along the blank wall of the convent, past three extraordinarily handsome 17th-century mansions, which make this the most impressive corner of town. Wander down this street to the **Catedral**, where de Lugo is buried behind the altar, and the **Iglesia de la Concepción**, which dates from 1502. Its font was used to baptise converted Guanche leaders. In Calle San Agustin it is possible to see the interior of a mansion, at Casa Lercaro, home to the **Museo de Historia y Archivo Insular** (open Tues–Sun 9am–7pm; admission fee, Sundays free). This fine building, with wood floors and its own small chapel, was built by the Genoan Lercaro family of bankers in 1593, the owner's first son, Francisco, becoming the Lt-Governor of Tenerife. The building is an ideal setting to lay out five centuries of the island's history.

From the Plaza del Adelantado, Calle Nava y Grimón leads past the peach-coloured walls of the **Convento de**

La Laguna locals

Santa Clara de Asis, the town's other immense convent, to the Convent of San Miguel de las Victorias Franciscanes. Here, the **Real Santuario del Santísima Cristo de La Laguna** contains a figure of Christ commissioned by de Lugo from a Flemish sculptor in 1520. Dripping with New World silver and gold, it is the most venerated figure in the town.

Two major museums are within reach of La Laguna. On the outskirts of the town is the **Museo de la Ciencia y el Cosmos** (Calle Via Láctea s/n; open Tues–Sun 9am–7pm; admission fee, Sundays free). This hands-on museum is an introduction to the wider world cosmology and the planets. The other is the excellent **Museo de Antropología de Tenerife** in the Casa de Carta in Valle de Guerra (Carretera Tacoronte-Valle de Guerra s/n; open Tues–Sun 9am–7pm; admission fee, Sundays free). This museum of popular culture is beautifully laid out in the 18th-century mansion, and depicts five centuries of rural life on the island.

The fertile Valle de Guerre is a centre for flower growing. Looking down on it is the **Mirador de El Boquerón**, where a map shows the distribution of agriculture, of bananas, avocados, potatoes, vines and the bird of paradise flower, which has become a symbol of the islands.

To the east, beyond the villages of **Tegueste** and **Tejina**, is **Bajamar**, a small, old-fashioned resort where people from La Laguna come to soak in the sea-water pools douched by the pounding Atlantic. Beyond it is **Punto Hidalgo**, a good place for coastal walks, which are signposted from the roundabout at the end of the town. The flower-covered Café Melita on the way into Punto Hidalgo has wonderful cakes and pastries, and views over the sea.

The Anaga Hills

The best view of La Laguna is from the **Mirador Jardín** in the **Monte de las Mercedes**. Looking down on the town and both coasts, it has a helpful explanation of where the lagoon was and how it gradually faded away. Listen for canaries in the trees and bushes. You might glimpse one, but they are not as bright in the wild as they are in captivity.

The Anaga Hills

Las Mercedes forest is the start of the **Montañas de Anaga**, a series of volcanic hills rising to 1,000m (3,300ft) with deep valleys running down to the sea, ending in small beaches accessible only by boat or after hours of walking. The best place to begin is beyond the Jardín at a second mirador, **Cruz del Carmen** at 920m (3,018ft), though the thickets of heather and fern give less of a view. Here is the Visitor Centre (open daily 10am–6pm) for the **Parque Rural Anaga**. There is a small exhibition about the local natural history, and an information point can suggest walks. Just beyond Cruz del Carmen a turning to the right leads to the **Mirador del Pico del Inglés**, one of the best viewpoints on the island. The road continues to wind through the hills. After El Bailladero, beneath which the north–south road tunnels, it becomes little more than a single track wandering all the way to **Chamorga**, a one-bar community at the end of the road.

The road north of El Bailladero leads through **Taganana**, a community of white houses and palms, which in 1881 felt so cut off it declared itself independent. Its 15th-century church is one of the oldest on the island. Beyond it is **Playa San Roque**, where surfers gather on the small beach in front of the buzzy Bar Playa Casa Africa. Further on is a string of restaurants at **Roques de las Bodegas**, and at **Benijo** the road dissolves into paths heading over the cliffs.

The dense vegetation of these hills includes the largest natural laurel forest in the Canary Islands, their leaves often dripping with moisture from the misty climate produced by the Trade Winds. Their prehistoric ecosystem supports bay trees, holly, heather and spurge, while the damp climate keeps alive the ferns, lichen and moss. There are also a number of cave houses here, such as those at **Chinamada**, where one of them has been turned into a bar and restaurant called La Cueva.

Walking in the Anaga Hills

Walking is the best way to explore the Anaga Hills. A starting point is the Visitor Centre at Cruz del Carmen, or the Alberguo Montes de Anaga *(see page 127)*, where you can obtain maps of the *senderos* (paths). Several walks begin around Las Carboneras, including one down to the sea at Punto Hidalgo, passing through three identifiable ecosystems. A more dramatic walk is from Chamorga at the end of the road down to Faro de Anaga, the lighthouse on the northeastern tip.

THE NORTH COAST

The fertile Orotava Valley made the Guanche tribe here the wealthiest on the island. It did the same for the colonisers who made the most of the ideal growing conditions, building impressive mansions on the proceeds. Villa Orotava, as La Orotava was then called, was a gateway up to El Teide. Just below it, where the valley arrived at the sea, was Puerto de Orotava, a handy port from where wine and other products could be shipped abroad. But in 1706 a volcanic eruption destroyed the north coast's major port of Garachico. Overnight Puerto de la Orotava's fortunes increased, and the port was re-named Puerto de la Cruz as a sign that it would do business with the whole island. When tourism started, this part of the island was where the curious visitors came, for the climate, the Botanic Gardens, the architecture and for

The coast around Puerto de la Cruz beneath El Teide

Playa Jardín, Puerto de la Cruz

El Teide. By then Alexander Humboldt had paid a visit and made his pronouncements. A mirador between La Orotava and Puerto de la Cruz marks the spot where the German naturalist expressed his delight in the view, though he was not so delighted when he returned from his trip up to El Teide to discover that his porters had abandoned the plant and mineral samples he had collected, because they thought them unnecessary ballast. It was not long before other botanists and natural philosophers were making the journey up the mountain, followed by the first holidaymakers, and when the Grand Hotel Taoro was built in 1892 it was the largest in Spain.

Puerto de la Cruz

The island's oldest resort has a population of 40,000 and a gentle air, with handsome buildings, a small fishermen's quarter and one of the most romantic seafronts in the world. Gently lit at night, the promenade wanders beneath palm trees, beside black rocks and beaches where white-crested waves pound reassuringly. From the black beaches of Playa Jardín to Playa Martiánez and beside the tropical oasis of Lago Martiánez, the seafront is a delight at any time of the day. The heart of the town is just inland from the harbour around the **Plaza del Charco de los Camarones**, named after a pool full of shrimps, that was once here. There are café tables, kiosks, bands and the general hum of the town's life.

On the east side Calle Quintana leads to the 16th-century **Ermita de San Juan Baptista** and the 18th-century **Iglesia de San Francisco**, effectively one church with the dividing wall removed and a medley of paintings of the Madonna. Opposite, the area once occupied by the Franciscan monastery is a place for concerts and other cultural events.

The street continues up past two handsome mansions with elegant patios and balconies, now the hotels **Monopol** and **Marquesa** (*see page 130*). The Monopol, dating from 1742, was the birthplace of Agustín de Bethencourt y Molina, founder of the Madrid Civil Engineers' School and General Director of Ports and Roads for Alexander II of Russia. The Marquesa, more elegant still, has pavement tables that are ideal for people-watching. In front of them the street opens into the Plaza de la Iglesia and the town's principal church, **Iglesia de Nuestra Señora de la Pena de Francia**, built in 1697 with a tower added in 1898. The organ was made in London.

The Harbour

The harbour today is small with little activity, and it is hard to imagine it as a stopping point for transatlantic trade. On one side is an artesanal craft shop, on the other the distinctive **Casa de la Real Aduana**, the former customs house and residence of the royal tax collector. To the west is **La Ranilla**, the fishermen's part of the town, where the seafront is an

Plaza Pérez Galdós, named after the Spanish playwright and novelist who was born in Gran Canaria in 1843, is the most pleasant square in La Ranilla. Stop here for a drink or *tapas* at one of the small restaurants or bars.

Toucan at Loro Parque

expanse of prime land that has been waiting a considerable time for the development of some kind of park. Because of the potential damage from the Atlantic, land directly on the seafront is not always regarded as prime building site. In La Ranilla's Calle El Lomo there's a small Archaeological Museum of Guanche ceramics. At the far end of La Ranilla beyond the football ground and municipal swimming pool is the 17th-century **Castilla San Felipe**, sometimes used for exhibitions. It marks the start of the town's main black beach, **Playa Jardín**, which is attractively landscaped behind. At the far end of the beach is Punta Brava and **Loro Parque** (open daily 9am–6pm; admission fee), one of the island's big attractions, with an orchidarium, aquarium, dolphin and sea lion shows, an 'African market' and what is claimed to be the largest collection of parrots in the world.

The Promenade

On the eastern side of the port, behind the customs house, is the **Plaza de Europa**, a fake castle with genuine cannon, built in 1992 on top of a very handy central car park. In one corner is the town's main **tourist office**. The streets behind the square are thick with handsome 18th- and 19th-century mansions with fine doorways and balconies. These lead to the promenade beside the small, rocky San Telmo beach where pools have been cut in the rocks for swimmers. The little white **San Telmo chapel**, dedicated to the patron saint of seamen, was built in 1780 on the site of a coastal battery.

The point of land beyond here has been laid out for the enchanting **Lago Martiánez** (open daily 9am–5pm; admission fee), one of the great attractions of the town. It was designed by César Manrique (1919–92), the artist from Lanzarote who did so much to promote the islands' natural resources. With palms, boulders and sky-blue swimming pools, this wonderful area compensates for a lack of really good natural swimming facilities in the town. There is a café and restaurant in the complex, and it is easy to spend a day here. The promenade, where Africans braid hair and sell carvings, bags and other leather goods, opens up as it reaches **Playa Martiánez**, the town's other beach that looks towards the cliffs rising to the east.

Lago Martiánez, designed by Canarian artist César Manrique

Jardín Botánico

At the back of the town is the **Jardín Botánico** (open daily 9am–7pm, 6pm in winter; admission fee) properly known as Jardín de Aclimatación de La Orotava. It started life in 1788 as a staging post between the New World and Europe, allowing tropical and sub-tropical plants to become used to cooler temperatures. The pamphlet that comes with your entry ticket gives a layout of the garden and its species. As a scientific institute, it is especially dedicated to the flora of the Canary Islands, with more than 30,000 specimens.

The **Parque Taora**, a landscape of gardens and ponds around the **Casino Taora**, is also a botanic delight.

Just beyond the Botanic Garden is the **Ábaco Casa Museo**, a beautiful 18th-century country house reconstructed with period furniture and a bounteous kitchen. One of its rooms has a quote from Robert Burns on the ceiling beams. Visits include a show of Canarian song and dance, plus a video. The bar and restaurant are open in the evenings.

Further diversions include the **Bananera El Guanche** tropical farm (open daily 9am–6pm; admission fee; a free bus goes from Hotel Atlantis throughout the day). This gives an insight into the island's agriculture; fruit and plants are on sale. **Oasis del Valle** (open daily 10am–5pm; admission fee) is another jaunt by exit 33 of the motorway, offering donkey and camel rides, a zoo and botanic garden. **Pueblochico** (open daily 9am–6pm; admission fee) by exit 35 is a small park with some of the island's buildings in miniature.

La Orotava

The historic centre of Tenerife's most attractive town is unsignposted, and visitors by car may find themselves going round in circles several times before they make it right up to the top right-hand side of the town where the island's wealthy landowners and merchants established their mansions. **La Orotava** is high above sea level and its streets are steep. Follow the 'Parking San Agustín' sign.

The church of **San Agustín**, which belonged to a former monastery, has a beautiful wood ceiling and a handsome retable. It sits at one end of the Plaza de la Constitución, where there is a little outdoor café kiosk, and is overlooked by **Liceo de Taoro**, a private club, and the adjacent **Jardínes Marquesado de la Quinta Roja**. These formal gardens were laid out in the 19th century around the mausoleum of the Marquis – membership of the masons

La Orotava, overlooking the coast near Puerto de la Cruz

Casa de los Balcones

precluded him from a burial on consecrated ground. More lush are the **Hijuelo del Botánico** gardens just beyond.

The tourist information office is in the bottom corner of the square in Carrera del Esculter Estévez. This street leads past the **Ayuntamiento** (town hall), an imposing neoclassical building which gives a clue as to how important La Orotava once was. The square in front of it is brilliantly decorated at Corpus Cristi *(see page 95)* using different coloured earth, sand and volcanic cinders. Beyond here, buildings give a sense of the riches that once flowed through the town. At the top of this road is the island's most famous domestic building, 17th-century **Casa de los Balcones**, which, as its name suggests, has superlative wood balconies. For many years it has been associated with the island's lace making, and there are 11 other outlets with the same name on the island. Staff in traditional costume will show you the best of the island's wares. Otherwise you can explore the beautiful patio and, for a small fee, the period rooms upstairs, peopled with dummies in costume, including a tourist and a granny sound asleep in her bed.

Casa del Turista, the mansion opposite Casa de los Balcones, is almost as grand, and is part of the same outlet for island ware and lace. A few metres further up on the right is the Hospital de la Santísima. Step inside the courtyard to see the revolving drum on the main door via which abandoned babies would be left in the care of the hospital's nuns. Worth visiting, too, is the **Museo de Cerámica** (open Mon–Sat 10am–6pm, Sun 10am–4pm; admission fee) in Casa Tafuriaste, a studio and showroom with a collection of traditional Spanish ceramics. Here you will learn how cracked pots were mended by stapling them with the spokes of umbrellas.

Town Church

Below these old streets is the **Iglesia de Nuestra Señora de la Concepción**, La Orotava's main church, built in the 16th century and rebuilt after devastating earthquakes in 1705, and retaining the original marble altar. Further down the hill is the **Museo de Artesanía Iberamericano** (open Mon–Fri 9.30am–6pm, Sat 9.30am–2pm, closed Sun, admission fee), which has an intriguing collection of ceramics, basketwork, instruments and furniture from all over Latin America.

Opposite is the 17th-century **Casa Torrehermosa** which sells a selection of crafts, backed by the local government. There are several good restaurants in and around La Orotava, such as Sabor Canario and La

> 'Around Orotava is the finest, most fertile land in these islands, and even in the whole of Spain, because on it can be grown and bred anything you may desire.' – Fray Alonso de Espinosa (1594)

Victoria, which offer further opportunities to check out the interiors of these picturesque mansions.

The Wine Lands of Tacoronte

East of Puerto de la Cruz, above the motorway on a pleasant rural road, are the villages of **La Mantanza de Acentejo** and **La Victoria de Acentejo**, scenes of the decisive battles between the Guanche *mencey* (chief), Bencomo, and the Spaniard Alonso Fernandez de Lugo. Matanza (the slaughter) is where 1,200 Spaniards were caught in a trap on 31 May, 1494. Only 200 escaped, de Lugo among them. He returned with a larger force the following year to win a decisive victory a short distance away at La Vitoria de Acentejo on Christmas Day 1495. Some 2,000 Guanche were slaughtered. It is difficult to imagine such scenes of carnage in these quiet hills.

Acres of vineyards mark this region out as **Tacoronte-Acentejo**, the best of the island's seven DO wine regions, *(see page 102)*. Just beyond La Matanza, the road goes under the motorway to arrive at the **Casa del Vino La Baranda** (open Tues–Sat 11am–8pm; wine tasting and shop till 10pm; Sun and public holidays 11am–6pm; free), just before enter-

Casa del Vino, El Sauzal

ing El Sauzal. This 17th-century estate is an attractive collection of buildings that includes a wine press and museum with detailed displays in both Spanish and English about viniculture on Tenerife. It is an impressive story, and the number of different bottles on display – *tinto, rosado* and *blanco* – may come as a surprise to anyone who has been

San Pedro, El Sauzal

searching for a selection of Canary wines on restaurant menus. The House of Wine has its own bar and restaurant and a room for sampling and buying wine. To further delight the palate, visit the **Casa de la Miel** (House of Honey) also on the La Baranda estate and run by the island council as a centre for extracting and bottling honey.

High above the rocky coast, best seen from La Garañona mirador, **El Sauzal** is set on a slope, and the square outside the town hall teeters down attractive steps beside a waterfall. **Tacoronte**, too, is way above the sea, and as may be expected it has a number of *bodegas* and restaurants. Its historic main square, Plaza del Cristo, is overlooked by a 17th-century church and convent of the same name, and at Corpus Christi coloured earth and flowers carpet the square. Ten minutes' walk down a steep hill is the church of **Santa Catalina**, with a typical balcony. It has two of the finest retables on the island and among its paintings is a fine *Inmaculada* by José

Luján Pérez. The coast at Tacoronte looks tantalisingly close, but the journey down is steep and winding. **Mesa Mar** has a small beach and bars. Just beyond, along a pleasant coast road, is **El Pris**, a small bay with fish restaurants.

West of Puerto de la Cruz

The motorway west of Puerto de la Cruz peters out at **Los Realejos**, which it divides between the older, upper part, Realejo Alto, and the lower, modern town, Realejo Bajo. This is the last chapter in the subjugation of the Guanches, where de Lugo pitched camp in 1498 and accepted the surrender of the remaining indigents and their lands. The much renovated church of Santiago Apóstol in the upper town still has the font where the converted Guanches were baptised.

Beyond Los Realejos is **San Juan de la Rambla**, an attractive small white village by the sea. Inland, high above it, is La Guancha, a quiet artesanal village with fine views.

Icod de los Vinos is on the tourist map for its dragon tree, **El Drago Milenario**. Reaching 17m (56ft) with a 6-m (20-ft) circumference, it is the largest and most ancient on the island. It stands by the main road on the west side of the town, helped in its old age by metal and concrete supports.

The Dragon Tree

The dragon tree (*Draecana draco*), which dates from the prehistoric Tertiary period, is unique to the Canary islands. It held a mystical quality for the Guanches, who saw it as a symbol of fertility and wisdom, using its bark on their shields when they went to war. Its resin, known as dragons' blood, turned red on contact with the air, and was used to embalm the Guanche dead. In Europe other uses were found for it, to dye hair golden, to stain marble red and to varnish violins.

Hard to date, it may not be quite the 1,000 years old that it claims to be. Near the small park in which the tree stands is **Mariposario del Drago**, a tropical garden full of butterflies from all over the world.

The old town of Icod is one of the most attractive on the island. Its typical buildings are best around the Plaza de Constitución, shaded by palms, oleander and jacaranda, and in Plaza de la Pila, where the 19th-century Casa de los Cáceres is used as an arts and exhibition centre. Icod has long been the centre of a wine producing area, and you can buy

The dragon tree at Icod

some of its wares at the Casa del Vino in Plaza de Constitución. The wine tasting festival takes place every year on the eve of St Andrew's Day (29 November), when locals ride on wooden sleds down the steep cobbled streets of the town making as much noise as possible, in remembrance of the wine barrels once taken down to the port for export.

In a little square below the Plaza is the church of San Marcos, which contains a sacristy and small museum. Among its treasures is a filigree cross made of Mexican silver weighing 47kg (104lb). Pinewoods behind the town stretch up towards El Teide. On the coast **Playa San Marcos** has an attractive small black beach with fishing boats and restaurants, and is a good place to drop in for a swim.

EL TEIDE

The traditional path up to El Teide (it rhymes with 'lady') for early visitors to the island was from La Orotava. They would be taken by guides with mules up the track used by pumice miners and by the *neveros*, who brought ice down from the mountains to make ice cream. Today there are four main roads up to the **Parque Nacional de las Cañadas del Teide**, so wherever you are on the island it is always accessible. Unless you are up for a five-hour climb, the last part of the journey has to be made by the Teleférico (cable car), 1.6km (1 mile) north of the Parador hotel and 8km (5 miles) south of the Visitor Centre. It does not operate in windy weather. You should arrive early in the morning to avoid queues. The highest mountain in Spain is 3,718m (12,198ft) above sea level and it is cold. Snow caps it for most of the year and temperatures can be well below freezing point. Yet it is still surprising to learn how many of the 2.5 million people who visit the park each year turn up in beach wear.

> Since the 1966 movie *One Million Years BC*, starring Raquel Welch, El Teide's bleak lands have made an ideal backdrop for a number of science fiction films.

Most people who alight from the cable car do not want to stroll far, and those who are pregnant or suffer from coronorary or respiratory problems should not attempt to do so, as there is 50 percent less oxygen in the air than at sea level. It is possible to walk just beneath the crater. It is also possible to walk on its rim, but to prevent erosion from hikers' boots, the authorities have introduced a system whereby you have to have written permission to do this. Permits can be obtained free from the Parque Nacional de las Cañadas del Teide on the fourth floor of Calle Elimio

Calzadillo 5 in Santa Cruz (tel: 922 290 129; open Mon–Fri 9am–2pm; <www.teleferico-teide.com>). You will need to take your passport and you will also need to show your free summit permit on the mountain top.

The Cañadas

El Teide rises from a great hollow in the centre of the island, a caldera, or cooking pan, that is the remnants of an earlier, much larger volcano, of around 4,800m (16,000ft). This flat, pale expanse between the remnants of the former crater wall and the peak of El Teide forms the park. In fact there were two earlier volcanoes, creating two calderas, separated by the mauve and pink barrier of Los Roques de García. Together they form an egg-shaped area 15km (9 miles) across. Lava and ashes have spilled from the volcanoes in a series of eruptions at different times, which ex-

El Teide, Spain's highest mountain

Early risers make for the summit of El Teide

plains why the rocks are so varied in texture and colour. Some cooled quickly into jagged formations, others cooled slowly into smoother, more liquid shapes.

El Teide lies to the north of the park and volcanic activity continues around the parasitic cones that sprouted around it. The most recent eruptions have formed a caldera on the summit of El Teide where fumarols – escape hatches for steam – still blow. In 1798 an eruption created Las Narices de Teide (Teide's nostrils) on the south flank. The most recent eruption from these peaks was in 1909 from Montaña Chinyero in the west of the park, and El Teide is considered to be still active.

Pico Viejo (3,134m/10,282ft) is to the southwest of El Teide and was formed a little earlier. A number of other volcanic peaks rise from the solidified lava in the park. To the north are the large caves of Cueva del Hielo or Cueva de los Cazadores. The highest point on the rim is Guajara (2,717m/8,914ft) on the south side of the Parador, and beyond it is the Paisaje Lunar, a haunting lunar landscape. Around Guajara Pass, which once linked the Orotava road with Vilaflor, are former Guanche huts and many of the island's mummies have been found in caves nearby.

The Routes into the Park

Once fertile lands scattered with small lakes, the calderas were the summer pastures for the Guanches' sheep and goats. They entered the region through *cañadas*, the breaches in the rim of the calderas that give the park its name. These are most visible on the southern side where the Llano de Ucanca is the site of a former lake. The four modern roads into the park rise steeply and there are few other places on earth where the landscape changes so quickly, from lush valleys to the rocky, volcanic terrain of the higher elevations, passing through a cloud level between 1,000 and 1,500m (3,300–5,000ft). As a result, there is a wide range of interesting flora.

Climbing El Teide Peak

The path to the summit around Montaña Blanca starts approximately 2km (1 mile) east of the Teleférico (cable car) base, where there is parking space for about a dozen cars and a map of the route. It is a straight walk up, with no scrambling or climbing, and it takes about five hours, during which you will climb around 1,400m (4,600ft). You can return via the Teleférico. A fleece and waterproof jacket are recommended, and in winter you should also wear snow glasses. Camping is not allowed in the park, but there is a refuge, the Refugio de Altavista, at 3,250m (10,650ft). Just beyond the refuge is a 19th-century ice cave, where early visitors cooled themselves after the horse ride up from La Orotava.

As the path reaches the top of the Teleférico, you will need to present your permit *(see page 52)* and passport to a ranger before continuing along the Telesforo Bravo path to the rim of the crater, through fumaroles emitting sulphurous clouds. The view is absolutely spectacular, and on a clear day you should be able to see all of the Canary Islands.

From the North

The road from La Orotava twists and climbs steeply through the moist Orotava Valley, past thatched barns and patches of agricultural land towards the village of **Aguamansa**, where there are forest trails through the pines and aviaries to take care of sick or wounded birds. This is in the cloud level, so if you plan to walk, prepare for some precipitation. Nearby is **Los Organos**, rock formations that look like organ pipes. Beyond Aguamansa look for another geological curiosity on the left of the road, the **Marguerita de Piedra**, a lump of basalt rock that seems to have exploded, forming 'daisy' petals. Finally, at 2,020m (6,630ft), it is joined by the road from La Laguna and it enters the park at the Portillo Pass.

The cable car

From the East

The road from La Laguna is also the best route from Santa Cruz, so it can be busy at weekends. Built in the 1940s by the military, this road is the straightest, least steep of the four, running along the ridge of the Cumbre Dorsal and providing spectacular views over both coasts. It passes through **La Esperanza**, known for its roadside meat restaurants. From here the **Bosque la Esperanza**, a forest of pines and picnic spots, spreads beside the road for a dozen kilometres. On the left, before the first viewpoint at **Mirador de las Flores**, is **Las Raíces**, the spot where Franco and a hundred co-conspirators met at an outdoor lunch in June 1939 to seal their agreements shortly before their attack on the mainland. A monument marks the spot.

At 2,400m (7,900ft) the road reaches two sky-watching institutions, the **Observatorio Meteorológico de Izaña** and the **Observatorio Astronómico del Teide**. Increasing light pollution on the island has affected the usefulness of the observatory (tel: 922 605 200; open to the public by appointment only Wed–Fri 10am–2pm).

The Starting Point

As the peak comes dramatically into view, the road from La Laguna meets the one from La Orotava at **El Portillo** just before the **Visitor Centre**. Moroccan cedars have been introduced here as part of an attempt to replant deforested areas. Measures to conserve the nature of the park have meant that many paths are closed to vehicles and hikers. Essential maps and guides should be on sale here, but don't count on them being in stock: if you are walking, it is best to try to find decent maps before reaching the park. Videos and displays give a good grounding into the history of the park and an idea of what to expect. Some tours and guides are advertised or may be available. You can check out the flora here: Teide daisies flower in the winter snow, pink broom blossoms in May, the Teide violet a little later. The rock's colour depends on the time of day and the light: the lava is in extraordinary hues of yellows, reds and browns, and there's the shiny black obsidian with which the Guanche made blades for their tools and weapons.

Cable Car and Parador

From the Visitor Centre it is about 12km (7 miles) to the **Teleférico** or cable car. It runs from 9am to 4pm, takes eight

View from the top

minutes, and stops 170m (560ft) short of the summit. Refreshments are available at both the top and bottom. Paths from the top lead to two miradors at the foot of the final ascent, for which you need a permit *(see page 52)*. From the viewpoints you can see the jagged rocky and rope-like formations from the mountain's latest lava flows.

The **Parador de Cañadas del Teide** *(see page 129)* is the only hotel in the park and it makes an excellent base for an early start to walk to the summit. The night sky is sparkling, and groups of visitors come to the Parador for dinner and astronomical talks. Near the Parador are **Los Roques de García**, extraordinary gnarled formations that are all that is left of the dividing wall between the two former volcanoes that make up the caldera. They are among the most photographed phenomenon in the park. Stones near these rocks are deep green from copper oxide, and are known as **Los Azulejos**, the glazed tiles.

From the Southwest

From Playa de las Américas, Los Cristianos and the other resorts of the southwest, the 90-minute drive up to the park starts either at Arona or at Granadilla de Abona and climbs steeply to where the roads converge at **Vilaflor**. Situated at an altitude of 1,400m (4,600ft), this village is the highest in Spain, and its population of 2,000 makes it the island's smallest municipality. It stands among volcanic cones in the middle of pine woods, of which the Pino Gordo, the fat pine, is the finest example, 65m (215ft) tall and 10m (30ft) in circumference. Vilaflor is a good base for exploring the mountains and is the nearest village to the park, where there are no shops or commercial outlets. Its 16th-century church was founded by a Catalan colonialist, Pedro Soler, who first put this land to work for the Spanish. Vilaflor is a popular stopping point, so if you are staying try to book a hotel in advance.

It is noticeably cooler here than on the coast and it snows in winter. Generally, however, when the weather is poor on the coast, it is sunny up here above the clouds. The bare earth on the tidy, geometrical terraces is covered with lava pebbles called *picón*, which helps to hold in the moisture. There is no shortage of water, and underground springs provide the island with bottled water. There is enough moisture for a healthy agricultural industry of tomatoes, potatoes and grapes. These must be among the highest vineyards in the world and their white wines are increasingly talked about.

Roques de García

Alpine flowers

Just outside Vilaflor is the **Ermita San Roque** with a mirador and the Restaurant El Mirador, which makes a good stopping place. There are two further miradors beside the road, **Mirador de las Pinos** and just beyond a large bottling plant, **Mirador las Lajas**. Both make pleasant picnic stops.

From the West

The road from the west coast rises from the white village of **Chio**, at 680m (2,240ft), from where there is a panoramic view back over the coast around the high cliffs of Los Gigantes. Less twisting than the road through Vilaflor, it climbs through the inhospitable, jagged clinker and dark grey lava to reach the road from Vilaflor at **Boca de Tauce**. Here a breach in the caldera rim lets the road through into the lunar landscape of the park.

THE NORTHWEST

The northwest of the island is one of its richest and most diverse areas. Deeply rural, it has many hidden corners as well as popular spots, none of which is ever very crowded. Much of the area is covered by **El Teno Rural Park**, a conservation area of more than 80sq km (30sq miles) based on the Teno massif, one of the geologically oldest parts of the island. There is a range of vegetation between the hills and valleys, and wild flowers are in abundance. Bird life is also very active, both in the hills and around the northern coastal plain, and sea birds can be seen from Punto El Teno. **Isla Baja** is the name given to the region that covers the districts of Buenavista, Garachico, Los Silos and El Tanque. Its capital is Garachico, which makes a good base. A number of traditional houses and *fincas* (country estates) throughout the region have been converted into places to stay.

Garachico

An hour before dawn on 5 May, 1709, the sky above **Garachico** was lit up by the eruption of El Volcán Negro, 8km (5 miles) inland. It was not long before two streams of lava were scorching their way through forests and vineyards towards the coast. Alarmed, the people of Garachico, Tenerife's principal port, watched it coming. Genoese merchants abandoned their mansions and monks and nuns left their religious houses, fleeing the path of the boiling lava. In the harbour, ships trading in sugar and wine could only put to sea and watch as the river of molten earth barged and burned its way through the town's buildings and filled up the harbour, turning the sea to a boiling cauldron. Garachico's days of glory were over, and it would never be the same again.

Castillo de San Miguel, Garachico

If you go up to the **Mirador de Garachico** you

can look down on the white buildings that cover the curve of lava jutting out into the sea and make out the paths of the two devastating rivers of molten rock. In the town itself there is a model of the catastrophe in the Isla Baja restaurant.

Garachico today is a handsome town of 6,000, with a Sunday craft market, and is so unhurried that it needs no traffic lights. Its seafront is given over to leisure, with a municipal swimming pool and a football pitch. Once or twice a year the sea comes in and batters the pitch to bits, though most days the blue water looks entirely benign, especially where it laps the black swimming rocks around the **Castillo de San Miguel**. With its bar and restaurant, this is a good place to look out across to Gomera as the sun goes down. The castle, dating from 1570, has a collection of shells from around the world, and provides a viewing point from its battlements.

Convent of Francis of Assisi

Just inland from the castle is the pretty **Plaza de Juan Gonzales de la Torre**, at the back of which the former land gate to the harbour has been excavated. There is a huge 17th-century wine press here, too, a reminder of the time when locally produced Malvasia wine made Garachico – and Tenerife – rich. Nearby is a monument to Cristóbal de Ponte, the Genoan banker who founded the town.

The parish church of **Santa Ana** is a few steps from the square. Rebuilt after the eruption, it contains a magnificent crucifix by Martin de Andujar, a Sevillian craftsman, and a figure of Christ made by Tarasco Indians in Mexico. Beside the church, the small curved Calle Esteban de Ponte follows the seafront. The de Ponte family house is here, and impressive buildings include the Isla Baja restaurant and El Jardín *pensión*,

Doorway in Garachico

which is opposite the tourist information office and Limonera craft shop.

The main square, shaded and with a refreshment kiosk, remains much as it must have looked before the eruption. A statue of the Venezuelan revolutionary leader, Simón Bolívar, has been added because his mother, María Concepción Palacio y Blanco, was born in the town. It was the first statue of the great liberator to be erected in Spain. On the north side of the square is the palace of the counts of Gomera. Dominating the western side is the 16th-century former convent of Francis of Assisi, its pristine white walls now housing the **Casa de la Cultura**, where exhibitions are held, and a small natural history museum. On the south side are the ochre walls of the Casa de Los Marqueses de la Quinta Roja. Now a beautiful hotel, with a bar and restaurant, it is also a centre of activities in the region, with information on walks and tours. Drop in to find out what is going on – and look out for the turtles in the garden.

Another smart hotel is the San Roque, in the Casa Noriega just to the west of the square, and its contemporary sculptures show the town's awareness of the arts as well as its heritage. A museum of contemporary art is housed in the 17th-century former convent of Santo Domingo. One other huge convent in the town is the 18th-century Franciscan convent, a closed order that still maintains around 15 nuns.

West of Garachico

The road heading west out of Garachico goes past the **Playa del Muelle** and up to a headland where the **Monumento a los Emigrantes Canarios** shows a figure with a suitcase and

Monument to the Emigrants

a hole in his heart setting off for a better life in America. There has been large scale emigration from this corner of the island, especially to Venezuela, and many towns and villages celebrate the day of Nuestra Señora del Buen Viaje, Our Lady of the Good Journey, on 31 August.

The nearest good beach to Garachico is a little further on, the **Playa La Caleta de Interián**.

As the road heads west, the countryside starts to flatten, smoothing a path first through sleepy **Los Silos** and arriving at **Buenavista del Norte**. Built around a central square with a small pavilion, its low, white houses have a languid,

southern feel. The church of
Nuestra Señora de los Reme-
dios was refurbished after a
serious fire in 1966.

The road from Buenav-
ista continues all the way to
Faro del Teno, the lighthouse at the northwestern
tip of the island where birdwatchers make for, on the
lookout for Barbary Falcon,
Cory's shearwaters and
ospreys. Road signs warn
motorists of the dangers of
landslides, especially in
windy and wet weather. La

Picturesque Masca

Gomera and La Palma are in view as you reach the headland, and at the lighthouse at **Punto del Teno** you can see
down the entire west coast.

From Buenavista the road heads inland, past vines and signs
for cheese for sale, and up through a changing mass of vegetation, with poppies lining the road. Among geological curiosi-
ties is the **Montañeta del Palmer**, which has been sliced like a
cake for the extraction of *picón*, a gravel made of lava which is
spread on agricultural land to retain moisture in the soil.

At the **Mirador del Baracán** there is a view down over both
coasts. Bees hum as they potter about the aromatic plants,
swifts dart overhead and there are paths off into the Teno Park.

Masca

The jewel of the northwest is **Masca**, a cluster of buildings
tipped over the side of the hill in a stunning setting above the
sea. Approached over the hills from Buenavista or along the
dramatic ribbon of road that flutters down from Santiago del

Teide, it is not much more than a hamlet. It has around 100 inhabitants and it was off the tourist map until the road to it was eventually constructed in 1991.

Near the roadside, where cars squeeze into the few parking spaces, there are a couple of restaurants with terraces where you can have cactus ice cream with goat's yoghurt and honey, or suck cactus and papaya juice through a straw while contemplating the steep walk into the ravine. Among the clutch of attractive buildings just below there is a small museum of local finds. Many people get no further than this but the adventurous arrive before 10am and head down the narrow **Barranco de Masca** to the beach, a six-hour round hike – two or three hours down, three or four hours back. It's a bit of a scramble in places, but the rock formations are truly dramatic, rising 600m (2,000ft) above the path that narrows to just a few metres wide. The reward is a rocky beach with a small pier, though the currents are strong and swimmers are advised to take care. It is possible to organise a connection with a boat to pick you up and take you to the port of Los Gigantes just down the coast, which is otherwise accessible only by going back to Masca.

El Tanque

El Tanque

El Tanque

The road above the coast at Garachico leads to **El Tanque**, a district of five hamlets scattered among pastureland in patchworks of fields between sweeping mountains. El Tanque is a small town overlooking the sea, centred on a corn exchange, the Casa de la Alhóndiga, that was once the town's meeting place. **Mirador Lomo Molino** (tel: 922 136 680) has good views, too, and, if you have time to stop, great food cooked by its students – this is a teaching restaurant.

It is something of a surprise continuing along this road to see blue-robed bedouins in camel trains. The **Camello Center** (Carretera General del Norte 4, tel: 922 136 191) has donkeys as well as camels for hire on half-hour excursions.

The road climbs up to the mountain pass at **Erjos** (1,117m/3,664ft), where paths lead down to old farmhouses in the valleys. This pass

Los Gigantes Harbour

divides north from south, and from here the full southern heat brings only cacti and *malpaís* to the dry scrubland. It meets the road up from Masca at **Santiago del Teide**, a sunny white town in a broad valley. To the east is **Montaña del Chinyero**, the last volcano to erupt on the island, in 1909.

The village of **Arguayo**, just beyond, is famous for ceramics and the **Taller y Museo Alfarero Cha Domitila** (open Tues–Sat 10am–1pm, 3–6pm, Sun 10am–2pm; admission fee) is a museum and workshop of traditional earthenware.

Los Gigantes to San Juan

Boats that sail to Masca bay are just part of the flotilla of pleasure craft berthed in **Los Gigantes**. This port, at the bottom of a steep hill, is the island's premier diving centre *(see page 84)* and the possibilities for water activities are endless. The port looks directly out at the *acantilado,* the cliff that rises sheer in front of it – this is the dramatic 800-m (2,625-ft) wall of the Teno massif, where the boat-less Guanche thought that the world came to an abrupt end. The cliff also drops fairly rapidly beneath the sea, making deep diving accessible.

The only beach in Los Gigantes is tiny, but there is a good swimming pool, Piscina la Laguillo, just up from the port. There is a much larger beach at its sister resort, **Puerto de Santiago** and **Playa de Arena**, which are within easy striking distance. These are all well developed, modern resorts on steepish hills that lack the boisterous nightlife associated with the bigger resorts further south. The next resort of **Alcalá**, also based on a fishing port, has natural pools to swim in. **San Juan**, 8km (5 miles) south of Los Gigantes, looks more like a working fishing port, with a friendly family beach around the harbour, though plans to build a fish packing factory beside it have met with opposition from the pro-tourist lobby. On Wednesday and Saturday mornings a food and craft market attracts visitors from around the region. There are also a couple of dive schools and some good fish restaurants.

Inland from San Juan is **Guía de Isora**, a rural community where potatoes and tomatoes grow. Its church has two Madonnas by José Luján Pérez.

> **The Atlantic Rowing Challenge, 5,000 km (3,000 miles) from Los Gigantes to Barbados, is one of the world's toughest sporting events. Boats 7.3m (24ft) long are rowed by two oarsmen. The race was inaugurated in 1997 by Chay Blythe, 30 years after his three-month trans-Atlantic crossing with John Ridgeway.**

Sunlounging in the South

THE SOUTH

Served by Reina Sofía airport, the south of the island is where it is hot, so this is where holidaymakers go, mainly to the resorts in the *municipios* of Adeje and Arona, in the merged touristopolis of Playa de las Américas and Los Cristianos. Hotels, apartments and villas continue to spread along the coast, bringing greenery to the *malpaís*, the badlands. Near the airport is the longest beach on the island, El Médano, where the steady trade winds attract surfers. All along the shore back towards Santa Cruz are rocky bays as well as small fishing ports such as Los Abrigos and Abona where fish is fresh on the menu. An upper road, from Granadilla de Abona to Güímar, where the Norwegian explorer Thor Heyerdahl discovered mystic 'pyramids', passes through some small villages with views all down the coast. Fifteen kilometres (10 miles) before Santa Cruz the road drops to the coast around Candelaria, the most important pilgrimage town in the Canary Islands.

The Big Resorts

You have to know where you are going when you arrive in **Playa de las Américas**. Built out of nothing in the 1970s, it has no natural centre or heart, the roads are often not sign-posted and directions are generally given by the names of hotels. If you are driving and try to head for the seafront to get your bearings, you will be disappointed. The seafront belongs to the four- and five-star hotels and the closest you will get to it is their car parks.

On the seafront you can see the spectacular hotel fantasies that make up various people's ideas of heaven, from Canarian

The built-up southwest coast resorts, near Fañabe

villages to Mexican *haciendas*, tarts' boudoirs and the glories of Rome. Most ambitious is **Mare Nostrum** *(see page 134)*, a 'resort' of five-star hotels that look like something out of a Cecile B de Mille epic. It includes the Pirámide de Arona, the Pax Romana congress centre with a restaurant where you can dine accompanied by opera or chamber music, and the Charlie Max Night Club. Mare Nostrum overlooks a small beach, the **Playa de Camisón**.

A larger beach, the **Playa de las Vistas**, lies between here and Los Cristianos but the main beaches of **Playas de Troya** and **Playa del Bobo** are on the north side

of the **Barranco del Rey**.
There is a tourist information point at this gully which
is near the rowdy **Veronicas**
strip, hub of more than 100
discos and nightclubs. Tech-
nically the *barranco* marks
the municipal boundary
between Arona and Adeje.
The coast north of here is
the Costa Adeje, which
drifts seamlessly into the
giant hotels of **San Eugenio**,

Watch the whales at Aquapark

Torviscas, Fañabe and **Playa del Duque**. The small harbour
of **Puerto Colón** in San Eugenio is the centre for all the
water activity, the boat trips, dolphin- and whale-watch
boats, and dive boats *(see page 85)*. Inland from the port is a
large **Aquapark**, just one of myriad activities.

There are no limits to the possibilities for entertainments
in and around Playa de las Américas, beyond simply eating,
drinking and dancing. Opportunities for spending money go
on around the clock; the seafront Thursday and Saturday
market at Torviscas is also open on Tuesday nights 6–10pm,
and you can go on sea-borne shopping excursions.

La Caleta just to the north of Playa del Duque is the last
resort to retain its identity. A meal in its excellent restaurant,
where around 40 dishes are laid out as in a market stall, so
you can just choose and point, gives a taste of real Tenerife.

Los Cristianos

The whole starting point of these resorts was the port of **Los
Cristianos**, which lies on the south side of Playa de las
Américas. They are separated by the volcanic cone of Mon-
taña Chayofila, but it is otherwise hard to see the join. The

port is still active, its ferries serving the neighbouring islands of El Hierro and La Gomera. The south-facing **Playa los Cristianos** and **Playa las Vistas** are sheltered and the sea is shallow and safe.

Los Cristianos has an authentic atmosphere, especially around its main pedestrian street, Avenida de Suecia, where there are inexpensive *pensións*, and above the Paseo Marítimo, where a row of small restaurants and bars offer sea views. Drop into the main old café, El Faro, opposite the bus station, to see photographs of what Los Cristianos looked like before the tourists came. Events and exhibitions are organised in the **Centro Cultural** where the tourist information office is situated. At the far end of the beach an open area is the site of a lively Sunday market.

The Municipal Towns

Inland, keeping a distant but watchful eye on their progeny, are the municipality's main towns, Adeje and Arona. **Adeje**, the former seat of the Guanche government, has never minded much how it made money. At the top of the town is

---

La Gomera

Christopher Columbus's last port of call before he headed into the unknown in 1492 was the island of La Gomera, now just 30 minutes away from Los Cristianos on Fred Olsen's Australian-built *Benchijigua*. When you step ashore at San Sebastián you will find yourself in quite a different world. This quiet, underpopulated island is just 24km (15 miles) across, but you need to get away from the port to find its rural secrets. At its centre is the Parque Nacional de Garajonay, a UNESCO World Heritage Site, which you have to pass through to get to the lovely Valle de Gran Rey. For the sunniest beach, take a bus to Playa de Santiago.

the remains of the **Casa Fuerte**, the stronghold of Pedro, Count of Gomera and one of the Genoese de Ponte family, who ruled the roost along this coast. He fell in with another rogue, the Elizabethan pirate John Hawkins, and together they conducted illegal trade with South America, as well as legitimately dealing in African slaves. Hawkins, who was later knighted for his role in defeating the Spanish Armada, was the first Englishman to become involved in the slave trade, in 1562. Wooden stocks in the Casa Fuerte are a re-minder of the time. The

In the port of La Gomera

town has a pleasant, if steep Rambla, lined with bars and cafés, that leads to the Iglesia Santa Ursula, with a Gobelins tapestry among its contents and an 18th-century chapel that was once part of a Franciscan convent.

Turn left at the top of the Rambla for the Casa Fuerte, and then up to Olivia, the café-restaurant at the entry point to the **Barranco del Infierno**, one of the most dramatic ravines on the island and the main reason that so many visitors come to the town. Stout shoes are needed for the round-trip walk up to the waterfall at the head of the *barranco*, which takes around three hours. There is a surprising amount of plant life along the way. If nothing else, this walk can give those stay-ing at the main resorts a flavour of the island's true nature.

Montaña Roja near El Médano

Along the South Coast

New developments continue around the southern tip of the island, at **Palm Mar** and the **Costa de Silencio**, which are entirely man-made communities. Between the two is **Las Galletas**, a thoroughly local little beach and port where fish are sold on the quayside every morning, including Sundays, bringing many *tinerfeños* in search of a good catch. The seafront is a pleasant stroll, with delicious Italian ice creams at Yo-Yo. At the Calibri restaurant you can eat fresh fish, *azul* or *blanca* (oily or white fish), by the kilo.

Perhaps the best place for fish restaurants is **Los Abrigos**, the next port along, where restaurants line the lane leading down to the port and hospitable women invite you in to dine. Restaurant Los Abrigos, right at the end, is bursting at weekend lunchtimes and its fish list is as long as your arm. Although these are pleasant little ports, neither is a real resort and accommodation is all but non-existent.

The longest beach in Tenerife stretches several kilometres around the **Montaña Roja**, a volcanic lump that punctuates the bleak acres of arid coast by the airport. Cars line the road but there are few amenities on the khaki-coloured sand, which stretches from the naturist beach of **La Tejita** to the small port of **El Médano**. Sunbathers should watch out for sunstroke in this blistering heat, but many of the people who come here are in search of good waves, for this is the haunt of serious windsurfers, and major championships have been held with the aid of the *alisios*, the steady northeast trade winds. There's just the one building that breaks the beachscape: the Playa Sur Tenerife *(see page 132)* has been catering to windsurfers for decades. El Médano, at the end of the beach, also has accommodation and restaurants.

Further along is **Poris de Abona**, a small community with a little beach.

Granadilla de Abona to Güímar

Just outside El Médano on the road up to Granadilla de Abona is the **Cueva del Hermano Pedro**, the cave where the shepherd boy Peter de Betancurt prayed as a child. Of Norman descent, Brother Peter was born on 19 March 1626, at Vilaflor. At 23 he left for the Americas where he became a missionary in Guatemala and did charitable work among the poor, for which he was canonised in 2002. The cave has become a pilgrim site.

The old town of **Granadilla de Abona** is being

Surfers off El Médano

A corner of Granadilla

spruced up. It can seem deserted after the clamour of the coast. There is an attractive hotel here, the Hotel Rural Senderos de Abona *(see page 132)* in a mansion dating from 1856, with a restaurant, El Terrero, open in the evenings. Clock chimes come from the church opposite, dedicated to St Anthony of Padua. A number of the houses in the old town are being restored, especially in Calle Arquitecto Morrero, just down from the church, where one has become a *casa rural*. Next door is the small **Museo de la Historia de Granadilla de Abona** (open Mon–Fri 10am–2pm, Sat 10am–1pm; free), a museum of local history. At the bottom of the street are derelict tobacco drying sheds; plans are afoot to turn them into a hotel and spa. There are several recommended walks in the mountains above Granadilla.

The upper road continues through sleepy old villages surrounded by terraced fields, many of them abandoned. At **Arico el Nuevo** there is also a sense of desertion, of pretty old buildings done up and awaiting some purpose.

The road dives in and out of a succession of deep gullies, the *barrancos*. Pigeons and doves of every colour appreciate the rocks for nesting, while the larger caves have been put to good use as storage space. At the **Mirador de Don Martín** there is a view over the Valle de Güímar where pineapple, avocado, banana, chirimoya, guava, cereal and vines grow.

Ancient Temples

Some of the dry stone terraces here, known as *molleros* or *majones*, look like the bases of pyramids and it is no surprise to find the **Parque Etnográfico Pirámides de Güímar** (open daily 9.30m–6pm; admission fee) above the town of Güímar. This park is the work of an extraordinary man, Thor Heyerdahl, who lived in Tenerife from 1994 until his death in 2002. In that time he discovered what he believed to be the Guanches' cult of building flat-topped, step-sided pyramids for sun worship. The ship-owner and fellow Norwegian, Fred Olsen, bought land for the park and helped to develop it into a research centre.

Through Heyerdahl's expeditions on the balsa raft *Kon-Tiki* and the reed raft *Ra*, he made connections between the civilisations of Egypt and Mexico. Several acres of buildings have been uncovered. Replicas of his rafts are on show, and the

Parque Etnográfico Pirámides de Güímar

links between the indigenous peoples of North Africa, the Americas and the Pacific are speculated upon in a museum.

Güímar is a working town of 15,000, known for its wines and with a number of traditional, male-dominated *tascas (see page 101)*, some of which lie behind unmarked doorways. It has two good churches, both with coffered *mudéjar* ceilings. The parish church at the top of the town has an exceptionally elaborate silver altarpiece, and the curiously arranged church of San Domingo, in the former monastery of the same name, is by the town hall in a shady square.

The tourist office is in the Casa de Artesana in Avenida de Obispo Perez Cácarez, the main shopping street, where you

Guanche chiefs, Candelaria

can pick up information on walks in the Malpaís de Güímar. This semi-desert wasteland surrounds the Montaña Grande below the town and spreads down to **Puertito de Güímar** on the coast. Here there is a pebble beach between the fishing boats, and outside the town, in the direction of the Club Náutico, is a sandy shore.

Candelaria

The name Candelaria, 'giver of light', means only one thing in the Canary Islands: a venerated Madonna, who is the islands' patron saint. The town of **Candelaria**, on the coast, is dominated by the 1950s basilica (open daily

7.30am–1pm and 3–7.30pm; free) that contains her image, and pilgrims gather by the thousand in the large square outside every August on the Feast of the Assumption, when the conversion of the Guanches to Christianity is re-enacted.

Souvenir of the Candelaria Madonna

Lining the sea side of the square are statues by José Abad of the seven Guanche *menceys*, or chiefs, who were in power at the time of de Lugo's conquest. Six of them didn't have too much to be thankful for when Christianity arrived. One, however, the *mencey* of Güímar, was already half way to becoming a Christian without realising it. Inside the church the story of the discovery of the Madonna and her healing powers is told in delightful but murky paintings. They show the wooden Madonna holding Jesus in one hand and a candle in the other, arriving on the shore in 1392. Two local shepherds discovered her, and one of them cut his hand on his knife while trying to ascertain if the statue was alive. The wound stopped bleeding the moment that he touched her. When news got out, the *mencey* of Güímar, who was the shepherd's leader, had a shrine built for the Madonna, and when the Spanish conquerors arrived, they convinced him that his conversion was underway. De Lugo was thus able to persuade him to join the Spaniards in their subjugation of the island's pagan Guanche tribes.

If you are visiting Candelaria, try to go on a Wednesday. From 10am to 3pm there is a large, bustling market covering the main square.

WHAT TO DO

Tenerife's highlights and attractions lie in its natural resources. With a pleasant climate and a diverse landscape of dramatic coasts and exotic interior, the island is ideal for all kinds of outdoor activities. Many visitors come here to walk in the hills and enjoy the abundant flora and search out unique fauna. Much of the island is given to parks and nature reserves. The sea, dropping steeply to the depths of the North Atlantic, is a favourite for both experienced and novice divers, and there are whales and dolphins to watch if you don't want to get wet. In the larger towns and resorts many entertainments and activities are laid on for visitors, too, from theme parks and medieval spectaculars to folk concerts and Canary Island wrestling.

OUTDOOR ACTIVITIES

Walking and Hiking

The island is crossed with the many paths that until comparatively recently were the only way of getting around the island. Today the Spanish Nature Conservation Institute ICONA has mapped *senderos turisticas* (tourist paths) and distributes free leaflets on walks in the Orotava Valley, the Anaga Hills and Teno Rural Park. More ambitious walkers, who have no coronary or respiratory concerns, will want to conquer the lavascapes of the *cañadas* around El Teide, and information can be found at the information centre for the Parque Nacional de Teide *(see page 52)*. Walking maps, guides and books, often in English, can be found in bookshops *(librerías)*. Cruz del Carmen Mirador has information

Windsurfer picking up the trade winds at El Médano

on walking in the Anaga Hills, where the Albergue Montes de Anaga *(see page 127)* makes a good base. Other hotels that make good bases for walking are La Quintana Roja in Garachico *(see page 131)* for the northwest and the Hotel de Alta Montaña in Vilafor for the southwest *(see page 134)*.

You can also plan walks before you go by checking out the website <www.teninfo.com/tenerife/senderos1.htm>.

Bikes and Karting

Mountain bikes can be hired in the main tourist centres, for example Mountainbike Active in Calle Mazarocco near the bus station in Puerto de la Cruz, tel/fax: 922 376 081. If you

Motorbikes can be hired

don't fancy all that pedalling over the mountains, go to Rafting Bike (tel: 922 725 875). Trips are downhill all the way, starting at 2,250 metres (7,400ft) and travelling 35km (22 miles) to the sea.

Motorbikes can be hired in the tourist centres. Dakar has outlets in Las Galletas and Los Cristianos. Bikes range from 50cc scooters (€30 a day) to 650cc models at €85 a day.

Quad bikes can be ridden in Quad Park in Arona, tel/fax: 922 725 176; <www. thequadpark.com>. At Quad Safari, tel: 922 714 596; <www.tenerife.com/quad/>, the excursions last from 45 minutes to 3 hours. The Quad Safari office is based in the Malibu Park commercial centre in Playa de las Américas.

Jeep Safaris are on offer in Playa de las Américas, and at Los Cristianos you can take a vertical trip with Balloon Experience (tel: 922 753 055).

Pomegranate flower

Flora Spotting

The island flora is one of the reasons for visiting Tenerife. It brightens the island throughout the year. May and June, when the roadsides are overwhelmed with flowers, are the best months to come, but there is something to see all year round. Flora endemic to the island can be found in many different habitats. Cañada del Teide supports alpine plants such as the Teide echium ('The Pride of Tenerife'), while desert-like species are found around El Médano in the *malpaís* lands of the south. Some of these are very rare, and no fewer than 19 have been identified as now being under threat.

When the islands were used as a staging post between the New World and Spain, many South American species were introduced. Some can be seen at the Jardín de Aclimatación de la Orotava in Puerto de la Cruz, sometimes called simply the Jardín Botánico. The Jardín Tropical in Playa de las Américas also has a substantial collection.

The Museu de la Naturaleza y el Hombre in Santa Cruz gives an account of the island's flora and its bookshop has several books and charts on the subject.

Further information can be picked up from the website <www.teninfo.com/tenerife/flora1.htm>.

Birdwatching

Birdwatchers should bring binoculars. The island is not abundant with birds, but there are some unusual ones that can be seen, particularly those unique to the island (*see Introduction, page 10*). Walking in the hills and forests of the national parks will be rewarding. Around the lighthouses on the three extreme points of the island (Faro de Teno, Faro de la Rasca and Faro de Anaga) you will find the best views of seabirds.

Look out for brochures or notices about organised local walks. Recommended books to take with you include: *A Birdwatcher's Guide to the Canary Islands* by Tony Clarke and David Collins, *Finding Birds in the Canary Islands* by Dave Gosney and *Where to Watch Birds in Tenerife* by Eduardo García del Rey. For a comprehensive list of birds that can be seen, visit the informative <www.eurobirding.co.uk/tenerife>.

WATER ACTIVITIES

Most water activities, from diving to whale-watching, take place on the west and south coasts, where just about every waterborne activity ever thought of occurs.

Swimming in the sea is relatively safe around the island on the designated beaches, but currents and waves can develop, creating powerful undertows. Look out for a red flag flown when conditions are unsafe for swimming.

Diving

The waters around the island swiftly drop to dramatic depths, with caves and caverns and a diversity of ocean life that have made Tenerife dive sites some of the most popular in the world. Sea temperatures are conducive year-round, from an average 20°C (68°F) in winter to

24°C (75°F) in summer. Barracuda, morays, sting rays, eagle rays and tuna are among the big fish; rainbow wrasse and trigger fish among the small delights. Sponges, anemones, and red and yellow gorgonias also lie in wait. Though the waters plunge to 2,000m (6,500ft), there is a legal depth of 40m (130ft) imposed on dives, many of which are multi-level. Operators offer courses from beginner to divemaster, with equipment and cameras available for hire, and video and film-making possibilities. Dive trials for beginners start at around €50 but

Kitesurfing is increasingly popular

note that Spanish law precludes under-16s from scuba diving. Most diving centres *(buceo)* operate on the west coast, with companies concentrated in Los Gigantes (Marina Los Gigantes Dive Center, tel: 922 868 002; <www.losgigantes marina.com/diving/diving.htm>), Playa San Juan, Los Cristianos and around the corner in Las Galletas (Buceo Tenerife Diving Center, tel: 922 731 015; <www.buceotenerife.com>).

Fishing
Game fishing: Shark, blue marlin, tuna and barracuda are the Big Game to be fished off the west coast. Boats can be hired in Los Gigantes (Punta Umbria V, tel: 922 861 918), Playa San Juan and Los Cristianos.

Whale and Dolphin-Watching

A number of attractive vessels offer whale- and dolphin-watching trips. The Canaries are on one of the principal migration routes for whales: one third of all species pass through the islands each year. *Nostramo* is a 1918 schooner that runs excursions from Playa San Juan, heading up to Masca. If you are lucky you may see a whale or dolphin, a turtle or flying fish. Nostramo also operates two glass-bottom catamarans out of Puerto Colón, the *Tropical Delfin* and *Royal Delfin* (<www.tenerifedolphin.com> freephone in Tenerife: 900 700 709). Another wooden sailing boat, *Katrin* based in Los Gigantes, will take you on a 'photo safari', mooring off Masca Bay, where you can swim from the boat and go snorkelling. Those who prefer to stay dry can take a ride on the *Golden Trout* 'Yellow Submarine' out of Puerto Colón.

> There is no shortage of high spots for hang gliders to jump from. Courses are available, for beginners and the experienced at the Parapente Club del Sur, Edificio Esmeralda 39, Callao Salvaje, tel: 922 781 357.

Windsurfing

All the windsurfers head for El Médano on the south coast, where the bay between the town and the Montaña Roja is one of the world's top 10 venues for the sport. The Playa Sur Tenerife Hotel, where you can hire boards, is one of the main places to hangout *(see page 132)*.

Horse and Camel Riding

There are a number of stables offering hacks through the countryside, including Centro Hípico los Brezos (tel: 922 567 222) near Puerto de la Cruz, with three-hour rides over the Tacoronte Hills on weekdays only. El Rancho Grande at

Camel rides make you feel closer to Africa than to Europe

Amarillo Golf (tel: 922 730 319) has horses for adults and ponies for children. Prices are around €15 an hour. Donkeys can be hired as well as camels at the Camello Center in El Tanque, in the northwest (tel: 922 136 191).

Golf

Spain's second oldest course, the Real Club de Golf de Tenerife, is the island's oldest, opened in 1932. Near Los Rodeos airport, with good views, it looks rather like an English park, and has an exclusive air. All the other courses are around Playa de la Américas in the south. Golf Las Américas, just by the resort, opened in 1998 with the accompanying five-star GL Hotel Las Madrigueras. Golf de Sur in San Miguel de Abona has hosted a number of tournaments. Also in San Miguel de Abona is the Amarillo Golf and Country Club. Las Palos Golf Center in Las Galletes, a nine-hole course, welcomes beginners. Green fees are around €30.

FOR CHILDREN

The seaside can offer much of what children want, though there is no perceptible tide and the land disappears into the depths very quickly. This means that there is little sea life in the rockpools and on the beaches.

The resorts are well supplied with play parks, rides, zoos and gardens. **Loro Parque** is a big day out, with an aquarium, dolphin, sea-lion shows, cinema and a large collection of parrots. Transport is provided from Puerto de la Cruz. **AquaPark** is a smilar propostion in Costa Adeje, with free transport from both Playa de las Americas and Los Cristianos. Primates star in **Tenerife Zoo** and Eagles soar in **Parque Las Aguilas**; both attractions are near Los Cristianos. There is a botanic garden and zoo, with camel rides, at **Oasis del Valle** in La Orotava. In Valle de Orotava,

Acrobatics at Loro Parque

Pueblochico is a model village of outdoor doll's-house sized Canarian buildings with botanic gardens and dragon trees in miniature. The **Museo de la Ciencia y el Cosmos** *(see page 36)* in La Laguna is a hands-on museum with lots of interest for children, as is the **Museu de la Naturaleza y el Hombre** in Santa Cruz *(see page 29)*. **Casa de los**

Science and Cosmos Museum

Cáceres is a doll and teddy bear museum in Icod de los Vinos near the famous dragon tree.

SPECTATOR SPORTS

Canary Wrestling

Lucha Canaria is a popular island sport which takes place in village halls and special *terreros* all round the country. It is played on a league basis, in which teams of 12 wrestlers fight individual bouts *(bregas)* in sand rings 10m (33ft) in diameter. The object is to force any part of your opponent's body to the floor using whatever means you can. Exhibition bouts are often staged as part of local fiestas when *juego de palo* or *banot,* a traditional stick-fight, is frequently also put on.

Football

Club Deportivo Tenerife is the island's principal football team, playing at the Heliodoro Rodriguez Stadium in Santa Cruz. A moderately successful side, the *blanquiazules* (the blue and whites) bounce between Spain's premier and second divisions. Games are generally played on Sunday afternoons.

SHOPPING

Many **designer shops** have outlets in the big resorts, but there is home-grown talent, too. In Puerto de la Cruz there are a number of fashion shops, including Cactus, at Calle Benjamin J. Miranda 1, which has beautiful pure cotton garments. Shoes are also relatively inexpensive and well designed. Spain is known for its well-made and inexpensive **leather goods**, from bags and belts to jackets and coats.

Embroidery and **lace-making** are traditional island crafts. Tablecloths and cushion covers with detailed patterns are a speciality. It is advisable to buy from a shop, such as the Casa de los Balcones in La Orotava, or one of its 11 branches, rather than from a street seller, whose goods are often made in Taiwan.

Island **craft** speciality shops include Artenerife beside the port in Puerto de la Cruz and Artesanas El Sol in Calle Nicoleas Estaveánez, Santa Cruz, where you can buy full Canarian costumes. Lava rock and obsidian is used in **sculptures** and a variety of **ceramics** are on sale. Pots are generally plain earthenware, many made in Guanche fashion. There are also copies of their fertility goddesses and die-stamps.

> Bargaining is expected in the flea markets and at street-side stalls run by the North African merchants, but beware of 'special offers' from these traders, whose goods may include ivory jewellery or leather or fur goods from endangered species. Not only will you be supporting the extermination of rare animals, but import of such items into Europe and the US is subject to heavy penalties.

Silver jewellery is worth looking at and **pearl** shops are a speciality. Tenerife Pearl has half a dozen outlets and a main building with an exhibition at

Armeñime on the main road between Adeje and Los Gigantes.

Cigars, hand-rolled from locally-grown tobacco, are a good buy. Souvenirs include giant ones 50cm long. Fancy cigarettes are also available, in pastel colours and prettily boxed. Volcanic gravel impregnated with perfume is a novelty – roll the cigar in it before smoking to sweeten the aroma of the fumes.

Local **wines**, hard to find abroad (or at the airport), make good souvenirs. Try to buy from the Casa del Vino La Baranda at El Sauzal. Tenerife **honey** *(miel)*

Straw hats

comes in various guises; there are handmade signs for it along the roadside. The best is from Las Cañadas del Teide – from bees that suck the nectar of white and yellow Teide broom. Find out all about the different kinds in the Casa de Miel by the Casa del Vino in El Sauzel. Other groceries to bring home might include jars of red or green *mojo*, *bien-mesabe* (*see pages 97 and 98*) or cactus, papaya and other exotic preserves.

NIGHTLIFE

As everywhere in southern Europe, much of the nightlife in Tenerife takes place on the streets. Canary Islanders need no clubs to find entertainment at night. Spontaneous chats in the squares and on the beaches, and dance music spilling out on to the pavements from the bars, are commonplace, and holidaymakers can join in the relaxation.

In tourist hotspots there are plenty of nightclubs and discos, as well as concerts, and little starts before midnight. As might be expected, **Playa de las Américas** has the most lavish nightlife on the island. Veronica's is the best known strip, with around 100 bars and discos that keep going until dawn. Some of the most extravagant shows are at Pirámide de Arona (tel: 922 727 549). Tropicana (tel: 922 710 878) also stages song-and-dance spectaculars. The Castillo San Miguel (tel: 922 700 276), signposted off the *autopista sur* at San Miguel, has medieval nights..

In **Puerto de la Cruz**, Victoria, Avenida de Colón, has been the most popular disco for more than a generation. Café de Paris at Avenida de Colónilla is a restaurant with dancing.

In **Santa Cruz**, KU, Avenida de Madrid, tel: 922 203 636, is a nightclub with a long-standing reputation. There's good music and dancing at El Convento, Tres de Mayo 73.

The **Auditorio de Tenerife** in Santa Cruz is the home of the admired Orchestra Sinfonica de Tenerife, whose concerts run from the beginning of October until the end of May. It is also the main venue for the island's opera and dance.

Where to Gamble

Casino Taoro (tel: 922 380 550) in Puerto de la Cruz is probably one of the best casinos in Europe. The Casino Santa Cruz is beside the Hotel Mencey in the city, which also has two bingo halls: Bingo Canarias at Carrer Imeldo Seris 9 and Bingo Siete Islas at Avenida General Mola 79. Playa de las Américas has a casino in the ground floor of the Hotel Gran Tenerife, with machines and tables. You will need your passport for entry to the casinos.

Night lights in Playa de las Américas

FESTIVALS

Fiestas are a part of island life, and there is a fair chance of seeing one during any stay – 30 days are officially set aside for festivals, based on the church calendar *(see page 95)*.

Carnaval

Undoubtedly the most spectacular festival is the pre-Lent carnival. Puerto de la Cruz and Santa Cruz are both completely overtaken by the event, which is said to rival Rio. Fired by a Latin American fervour, it requires the same inordinate lengths of preparation. Events last for nearly two weeks, starting with the election of a Carnival Queen and climaxing on Shrove Tuesday with the *coso*, the grand parade, with floats on various themes, and everyone in the fanciest carnival dress. There is a strong transvestite element and dancers are accompanied by *murgas*, groups singing satirical songs. The event draws to a close on Ash Wednesday with El Entierro de la Sardina (the burial of the sardine), a mock funeral attended by people in outrageous outfits, who beat their breasts and shed crocodile tears.

Corpus Christi

One of the most widely celebrated religous festivals on the island is the eight days (Octavo) of Corpus Christi at the end of May or the beginning of June. The best places to see it celebrated are La Laguna and La Orotava, where pavements are covered with spectacular carpets made out of flowers and a wide array of colours from volcanic sand. The procession that makes its way over them crushes the flower petals and fills the air with their scent.

Romerías

Corpus Christi marks the beginning of the Romería season of local festivals involving food, wine and dancing. Again it is La Laguna and La Orotava that put on the biggest shows, with, respectively, the Romería de San Isidro in mid-June and the Romería de San Benita a fortnight later. Arico, Granadilla, Güímar and Icod also have large Romerías during the month.

Local fiesta, local dress

Assumption

The biggest pilgrimage takes place on the day of the Assumption (15 August) at Candelaria, where the statue of Our Lady of Candelaria, patron saint of the Canary Islands, is paraded in the streets. On the day before there is a re-enactment of the appearance of the Virgin to the Guanche shepherds.

Festivals

For public holidays, see page 116.

January: *Cabalgata de los Reyes* (Procession of the Three Kings, Santa Cruz and Garachico), with costumes, brass bands, camel cavalcades.

February/March: *Carnaval*, Santa Cruz's extravaganza; also in Puerto de la Cruz.

March/April: *Semana Santa* (Holy Week): solemn pre-Easter processions in many towns and cities throughout the island.

April: local fiestas on 25th (Icod, Tegueste).

May: spring festivals, opera festival (Santa Cruz). *Fiestas de la Cruz* (all places with Cruz [cross] in their name): processions, festivities and fireworks. San Isidro (Los Realejos), San Isidro (Santa María de la Cabeza, with large firework display).

Fiesta de Corpus Christi (late May or early June, La Laguna, La Orotava and elsewhere); beautiful flower carpets.

June: *Romería de San Isidro* (La Orotava), *Romería de San Benito* (La Laguna); ox-drawn carts laden with local produce. Local fiestas (Arico, El Sauzal, Grandill, Güímar, Icod).

July: *Fiesta del Mar* (Festival of the Sea, Los Realojos, Puerto de la Cruz, Santa Cruz). *Fiesta de la Virgen del Carmen*, patron saint of seamen. *Romerías de Santiago Apóstol* (Festival of St James, Santa Cruz): pilgrimage, fireworks. Local fiestas (Candelaria, La Laguna, Los Realojos, Santiago del Teide).

August: *Fiesta de la Asunción* (Assumption, Candelaria): re-enactment of the appearance of the Blessed Virgin to the Guanches. Local fiestas (Garachico, Los Cristianos).

September: *Fiestas del Santísimo Cristo* (La Laguna, Tacaronte): floats, fireworks, sports, theatre and poetry. Local festivals (Güímar, Guía de Isora). Grape harvest.

October: Local fiesta (Granadilla).

November: *Todos los Santos* (All Saints Day). *San Andrés* (St Andrew's): new wine tasting festival in Icod, La Orotava and Puerto de la Cruz.

December: *Navidad* (Christmas). *Noche Vieja* (New Year's Eve).

EATING OUT

There is no shortage of restaurants serving chicken and pizza in the resorts, and Chinese restaurants are a popular alternative for *tinerfeños*. But any visitor should concentrate on getting to know the local dishes, which are the staple of most restaurants across the island. These are based on home-grown pulses and vegetables, fabulous fish from the Atlantic, and meat from indigenous animals. Portions are generally healthy, and establishments are usually relaxed, so you can be as picky as you like. *Cocina Canario*, *cocina casa linga* and *típico* are signs of local cooking. *Tapas*, small dishes to eat as appetisers, are served in many bars and restaurants and they can be made into a meal. And there are eminently palatable wines from the island's five recognised denominated regions.

Spices on sale at market

WHAT TO EAT

Vegetables

One of the mainstays of the island are potatoes, and the fact that they are called *papas* here, as they are in South America, and not *patatas*, as they are in Spain, is a clue to their affinities. There are no blights known to the local tuber, and there are a dozen regularly grown Andean varieties, notably *papa negra*, black potatoes. The size of squash balls and the colour of wood ash, they are usually prepared *arrugadas* or 'wrinkled', boiled in their jackets in highly salted water (traditionally sea water) and usually served with a *mojo* sauce.

Papas, the island's speciality

Mojo sauces, which accompany both fish and meat dishes, are made of olive oil, herbs and spices and come in two colours – red and green. These are either poured on to a dish or served in their own bowls for you to dip into or spoon out. Restaurants have their own recipes. The red *mojo picón* has dried peppers, chilli or paprika; the green *mojo verde* is made of parsley or, more distinctly, coriander *(cilantro)*.

Sweet potatoes, or yams, are also grown and can be seen piled high in the markets, but they are by and large absent from restaurant menus.

Another Latin American influence is corn cobs *(piñas de millo)*, used in soups and stews including *el pucho canario*, the major stew of the Canaries, in which a variety of local vegetables is likely to appear, such as chickpeas *(gabanzos)*, kidney beans and *bubango*, a particular kind of marrow.

Fried fish

Soups are plentiful and include *vieja ropa* ('old clothes'), a kind of *minestrone* into which anything goes, and *rancho canario*, a watercress soup.

Salad ingredients are generally fresh, as you might expect, and tomatoes are particularly tasty.

Gofio

If you eat anywhere on the island, it won't be long before you encounter *gofio*, the staple food of the Guanche. This is toasted ground corn, generally maize, but sometimes barley or wheat or even chickpeas, and it is served in a variety of ways. It can be added to soups as a thickener, and it comes as a seasoned broth, *escaldon*, usually served in an earthenware dish. It is also used as an accompaniment to dishes, or as a dessert, when it is made into a milk pudding *(frangollo)* or a mousse *(mus)* served with *bienmesabe* ('it tastes good to me') made from almonds and honey.

Meat

Tenerife is not a great meat eating land. There is beef and pork, but the principal interest lies in local goat *(cabrito)*, usually simply grilled, and rabbit *(conejo)*. *Conejo en salmorejo* is a stew of diced rabbit in a marinade, which is fried and boiled in its own juices and may be served with *papas arrugadas*. *Costillas con papas de piñas de millo* is a stew of pork ribs, potatoes and corn cobs.

Fish

Fish is the glory of the island. The deep cold waters produce meaty flesh with a lot of flavour. Even sardines, simply grilled, are delicious. Most visitors will have difficulty identifying many of these mid-Atlantic species, some of which do not exist in translation *(see below)*. Parrot fish *(vieja)* has such delicate scales that they are not cleaned for cooking, and you have to skim them off your plate, moving the knife up from the tail. In fresh fish restaurants larger fish is often sold by the kilo, when white fish *(blanco)* is slightly

---

Fish on the Menu

Many of the exotic Atlantic fish you will see on the extensive menus in Tenerife are unlike any you will see in most of Spain, and some are not easily translated. These include:

Abadejo – pollack; *aguja azul* – blue marlin; *bacalao* – cod; *chipirón* – baby squid; *caballa* – horse mackerel; *cabrilla* – grouper; *cherne* – sea bass; *choco* – cuttlefish; *congrio* – conger eel; *burro* – donkey fish; *corvino* – corb; *dorado* – gilthead bream; *lenguado* – sole; *merluza* – hake; *mero* – grouper; *morena* – moray eel; *pez espada* – sword fish; *rodaballo* – turbot; *salema* – gold-lined bream; *salmoneta* – red mullet; *same* – gold bream; *sarda* – mackerel; *sargo* – white bream; *vieja* – parrot fish.

Delicious fresh fruit

more expensive than oily fish *(azul)*. There are local mussels *(lapas)*, and the large prawns *(gambas)* make an excellent *tapa*.

A *cazuelo* (stew) of fish is a good way to sample what is available. This is made with a wide variety of fish in recognisable chunks, with some vegetables added. Portions are generous.

Fruit

The island's exotic fruits arrive on the table whole or in juice drinks. Bananas are mostly of the small Dwarf Cavendish variety, and are sometimes served for breakfast with fried eggs and rice – a Cuban speciality. Interesting fruit to try includes prickly pear, *chirimoya* or custard apples and *níspero*, small yellow medlars that ripen in May. Roadside stalls are one way to find them fresh.

Papaya, mango and prickly pear (cactus) are all in abundance and are turned into fruit juices.

Cheese

There are a number of local cheeses to try out, made from both goats' and sheep's milk and varying in strength from mild to tangy. Cheese is not universally available and if you see any advertised on your travels around the island, it is worth seeking out. Arico is a cheese-making centre.

WHERE TO EAT

Good restaurants are to be found along the main roads, as well as in the main towns. *¡Que Bueno!*, a book of top restaurants, is published every year, with text in both Spanish and English, though its entries tend to be skewed towards the swankpots of the Costa Adeje.

Tascas and Bodegas

Tenerife has a tradition of *tascas*, small eating houses where you can also go just for a drink. A number of these have become rather smart in Santa Cruz and elsewhere, with cutting-edge young chefs trying to make their mark. At the same time they are cozy places to eat. *Bodegas*, *bodegones* and *bodeguitas*, originally wine houses, are fairly indistinguishable bars with *tapas* and even full meals provided. Pick what you want from a menu: there is no formality about having to have courses in any particular order, or with any particular accompaniment.

Tinerfeños eat lunch, their main meal, around 2 or 3 pm, and dinner from around 9pm. A number of restaurants close on Sunday night and one day a week, often Monday.

Sign for fresh meats

WHAT TO DRINK

Tea and Coffee

There are plenty of places to drop in for a drink. Coffee is the leisure daytime drink of the island. As on mainland Spain, you can have *café solo* (equivalent of an espresso), *cortado* in a glass tumbler with a little milk, *café con leche* with milk and *Americano* or *largo*, a solo with extra water. Occasionally you may be asked if you want a black *(negro)* or brown *(marrón)* roast. Cafés often do deals for breakfasts, including juice and perhaps a roll or croissant. Cakes and pastries are usually on offer, but away from the main towns fresh bread is not always available until later in the day, and a doughnut or a half-frozen croissant may be all there is.

Tea is generally a bag in hot water, but the Folie Café, a wonderfully atmospheric little nightspot in Calle Santo Domingo, La Laguna, has pots of speciality teas.

Fresh orange and other juices are usually available and the local beer, Dorada, is a blond lager that will quench any thirst. Some of the more traditional bars don't have signs outside and you only know they are there when they are open.

Wine

Tenerife is the main wine-making Canary Island. Although it produces around 5 million litres a year, there is no guarantee that a local label will be on your restaurant wine list, but if it is there, you should choose it. House wines are often Riojas, which may be heavier than you want.

The island is divided into five *Denominaciónes de Origen* (DO), and because of the great difference in altitude, the grape harvest is staggered. If you are here on 29 November, the eve of St Andrew's day, make for the wine-tasting festivals in La Orotava, Puerto de la Cruz and, most entertainingly, Icod de los Vinos, where people slide on boards down the cobbled streets and make a racket with tin cans, echoing the barrel runs down to the former port.

Local rum *(ron)* is made from cane sugar.
Sweet liqueurs include *ronmiel*, made from palm sap, and *cobana*, made from bananas.

The **Abona** DO region in the south reaches right up to Vilaflor which must make the vineyards about the highest in the world. They produce mainly white wines from a dozen grape varieties, plus a few reds and rosés.

Valle de la Orotava covers the municipalities of La Orotava, Realejos and Puerto de la Cruz, and produces full reds and whites.

Tacoronte-Acentejo is the best known and most productive of the regions, making young reds from Listán Negro and Negromoll grapes. Brands include Viña Norte, which has 600 growers and has been winning

Casa del Vino, El Sauzal

prizes since the 1990s, and Humboldt Tinto, which won a gold medal at the Vinalies Internationales in Paris in 2003.

Ycoden-Daute-Isora has a long history of producing light, aromatic reds as well as whites.

Valle de Güímar produces white wines from white grapes, including the Gual and Verdella, grown between 600 and 800m (2,000–2,600ft).

There is also a substantial amount of fortified wine made from Malvasía or muscatel grapes. Wineries *(bodegas)* are generally places where you can just drop in, and if you book ahead, some will show you around. The best place to find out about the island's wines is the Casa del Vino La Baranda *(see page 48)*. Or visit <www.bodegasinsularestenerife.es>.

To Help you Order (in Spanish)

Could we have a table?	¿Nos puede dar una mesa, por favor?
Do you have a set menu?	¿Tiene un menú del día?
I would like...	Quisiera…
The bill, please	La cuenta, por favor

Deciphering the Menu

agua minerale	mineral water	**flan**	caramel custard
à la plancha	grilled	**helado**	ice cream
al ajillo	in garlic	**jamón serrano**	cured ham
al punto	medium	**judías**	beans
arroz	rice	**langosta**	lobster
asado	roast	**leche**	milk
atún	tuna	**mariscos**	shellfish
azúcar	sugar	**mejillones**	mussels
bacalao	cod	**morcilla**	black pudding
bocadillo	sandwich	**pan**	bread
boquerones	anchovies	**pescado**	fish
buen hecho	well done	**picante**	spicy
buey/res	beef	**poco hecho**	rare
café	coffee	**pollo**	chicken
calamares	squid	**postre**	dessert
callos	tripe	**puerco**	pork
cangrejo	crab	**pulpitos**	baby octopus
cerdo	pork	**queso**	cheese
cerveza	beer	**sal**	salt
champiñones	mushrooms	**ternera**	veal
chorizo	spicy sausage	**tortilla**	omelette
cocido	stew	**trucha**	trout
cordero	lamb	**salsa**	sauce
ensalada	salad	**vino**	wine
entremeses	hors-d'oeuvre	**verduras**	vegetables

HANDY TRAVEL TIPS

An A–Z Summary of Practical Information

A

ACCOMMODATION

a single/double room with bath/shower	**una habitación sencilla/doble con toilet/ducha**
What's the rate per night?	**¿Cuál es el precio por noche?**
Is breakfast included?	**¿Está incluído el desayuno?**

Don't expect to turn up at any place and find accommodation; most hotels and apartments are centred on the main towns and resorts. But the island is not large and it is easy enough to make a base from which to explore. The standard of accommodation is generally high and you are unlikely to have anything to complain about. Prices are reasonable and establishments are graded by a system that allows for many categories of accommodation and variations within each category. A hotel may be rated from one-star to five-star Gran Lujo (GL) which signifies top-of-the-range quality, but stars are not always directly reflected in the price. Most of the four- and five-star hotels are in the major southern resorts, and many offer deals. Santa Cruz de Tenerife and Puerto de la Cruz have a selection of lower-rated places. By law, prices must be displayed in hotel reception areas and in the rooms. Breakfast is not always included in the basic rate.

In addition to hotels there are apartments and 'aparthotels' where each room or suite of rooms has its own kitchen facilities yet retains all the trappings of a hotel. Apartments are graded with one to four 'keys', shown in symbols, depending on amenities.

Package holidays tend to provide accommodation in hotel complexes and self-catering apartments. Private apartments, of which there are a large number, are advertised in local papers by individuals and agents.

There are also an increasing number of country houses and hotels (*casas rurales and hoteles rurales*), usually in traditional houses or *fincas* (country estates). The tourist offices have details, or visit <www.ecoturismorural.com/canarias>.

If you plan to arrive during the high season (late November to February, July and August), book accommodation well in advance through a travel agent or directly with the hotel. *(For accommodation suggestions, see page 127.)* For a full listing of accommodation consult the Spanish National Tourist Office *(see Tourist Information Offices on page 123)*, or local tourist offices.

AIRPORTS *(aeropuertos)*

There are two airports on the island. International flights use Reina Sofía Airport (Tenerife-Sur) in the south (tel: 922 635 300). This is busiest on Tuesdays and Fridays. Buses run to Los Cristianos and Playa de Las Américas (about 25 minutes) and to Puerto de la Cruz, (1hr 40 min). The inter-island air traffic is handled by Los Rodeos (Tenerife Norte) airport near La Laguna, tel: 922 635 990).

B

BUDGETING FOR YOUR TRIP

To give you an idea of what to expect, here's a list of some average prices in euros. A euro is worth approximately £0.60p and approximately US$1.

Accommodation: Rates for a double room can range from as low as €25–30 at a *pensión* or *hostal* to as much as €360–420 at a top-of-the-range five-star hotel. A pleasant three-star hotel will cost in the range of €80. But rates increase during the high season, beginning around late November and culminating with the Carnaval.

Apartments: Per night for a family apartment prices range from under €30 for one key to more than €75 for four keys. Discounts are often available for bookings of a week or more.

Attractions: Most museums and gardens charge a minimal entry

fee of around €3. More expensive (around €10) are the larger attractions such as the Pyramides de Güímar and theme parks such as
Loro Parque.

Car hire: Around €35 a day

Meals and drinks: In a bar, a continental breakfast (fresh orange
juice, coffee and toast) will cost around €4. The cheapest three
course meal, *menú del día*, with one drink, in a small bar/restaurant
will be around €7. Dinner in a medium level restaurant will be
about €20 per person, including wine. At the top restaurants expect
to pay at least twice that amount.

Petrol: Around €0.65 a litre.

Sports: Golf green fees (per day) range from around €45–55.
Tennis court fees start at around €6 an hour. Horse riding starts at
about €12 an hour.

Taxis: State regulated and inexpensive, a taxi journey within a town
is unlikely to cost more than €3 or €4. The fare from Playa de Las
Américas to Reina Sofia airport is around €18.

C

CAMPING

Camping is not a common option on the island, and it is prohibited
in the national parks. There is a site on the south coast, Camping
Nauta Cañada Blanca in Las Galletas (tel: 922 785 118; fax: 922
795 016).

I want to change some pounds/dollars.	**Quiero cambiar libras/dólares.**
Do you accept travellers' cheques?	**¿Acepta usted cheques de viajero?**
Can I pay with this credit card?	**¿Puedo pagar con esta tarjeta de crédito?**

CAR HIRE *(coches de alquiler)* (See also DRIVING)

Normally you must be over 21, sometimes 24, to rent a car, and you will need your passport, a major credit card and a valid driving licence that you have held for at least 12 months. Cars are generally manual transmission, and you will have to hunt around if you want an automatic vehicle.

There are around 100 local car-hire companies – 25 in Santa Cruz alone – and these tend to be cheaper than the better known companies. If you hire a car before you leave home, especially via the Internet, it is also usually cheaper. Local companies include Amigoautos (<www.amigoautos.es>), Cicar (www.cicar.com) and Tenerife Rent a Car (www.trc-cars.com>). All the big international companies (Avis, Europcar, Hertz) have offices at the airports and in the major towns. Hotels can recommend local firms.

I'd like to rent a car.	**Quisiera alquilar un coche.**
for one day/week.	**por un día/una semana.**
Please include full	**Haga el favor de incluir el**
insurance.	**seguro a todo riesgo.**

CLIMATE

With a temperature of a fairly steady 22°C (72°F) year-round, sunshine is the rule, but the weather in the north and eastern parts of the island can be changeable. In spring there is a cold and wet gust from the northwest, and in autumn the famous hot sirocco raises temperatures. Remember that the island is on a parallel with West Africa, and the temperatures in the southern resorts and in the *malpaís* can be high, so be careful not to burn. Up in the hills, it becomes much cooler, even in the town of La Laguna, and the trade winds keep the northeast damp for most of the year. Temperatures drop to minus figures around El Teide's snowcapped summit and in the Cañadas.

CLOTHING

In addition to summer clothes and beachwear, don't forget a sweater or jacket for evenings. For excursions to high altitudes, you will also need warmer clothing and some sturdy shoes. Some protection from the rain may well come in handy.

Casual wear is the norm, although in five-star hotels, the best restaurants and the casino, a jacket and tie, though not obligatory, will not be out of place for men.

Topless bathing is quite common, and is acceptable at most hotel pools. Beachwear, shorts, bikini tops and mini-skirts should not be worn when visiting religious places.

COMPLAINTS

By law, all hotels and restaurants must have official complaint forms *(hoja de reclamaciones)* and produce them on demand. The original of this triplicate document should be sent to the Ministry of Tourism; one copy remains with the establishment involved and one copy is given to you. Try to resolve your problem before going through this procedure, as it will be difficult for you to succeed in any claims once you are off the island. However, the very action of asking for the *hoja* may resolve the problem in itself, as tourism authorities take a serious view of malpractice, and can revoke or suspend licences.

You should also inform the local tourist office, or in serious cases the local police, of any complaints and seek their assistance.

CRIME

Theft is only really likely in tourist areas. Never leave anything of value in your car. Use the safe deposit box in your room for all valuables, including your passport. Burglaries of holiday apartments do occur, too, so keep doors and windows locked when you are absent. There is some opportunistic bag snatching and pocket picking in busy places such as markets or at fiestas. But Tenerife does not have a high crime rate. You must report all thefts to the local police within 24 hours for your own insurance purposes.

I want to report a theft.	**Quiero denunciar un robo.**

CUSTOMS AND ENTRY REQUIREMENTS

Most visitors, including citizens of all EU countries, the USA, Canada, Ireland, Australia and New Zealand, require only a valid passport to enter Spain. Although Spain is in the EU, there is still a restriction on duty-free allowances at customs *(aduana)* when returning to the UK from the Canary Islands. This is: 200 cigarettes or 50 cigars or 250g smoking tobacco; 1 litre spirits over 22 percent or 2 litres under 22 percent, 2 litres of wine and £145 worth of goods.

D

DRIVING

Driving conditions. The rules are the same as in mainland Spain and the European continent: drive on the right, pass on the left, yield right-of-way to all vehicles coming from your right.

Speed limits are 120 km/h (74 mph) on motorways, 100km/h (62mph) on dual highways, 90km/h (52mph) on country roads, 50km/h (31mph) in built-up areas and 20km/h (13mph) in residential areas.

Motorways are toll-free. In the main towns, and even in smaller provincial ones, traffic can be heavy and one-way systems confusing, especially as roadsigns are woefully inadequate.

Parking: You are more likely to find a parking space during lunch hours (2–4pm). Consider parking at the edge of towns and taking buses or taxis to the centre.

Many roads are narrow and twisting. Always slow down when passing through villages. At any time you may come across a herd of goats, a donkey and cart, a large pothole, or falling rocks.

Petrol. Petrol stations on main roads often open 24 hours and mo... take credit cards. They are less frequent off the beaten track an... often close at night and on Sundays. Most hire cars take unleade... petrol, which in Spain is called *sin plomo*.

Traffic police. Armed civil guards *(Guardia Civil)* patrol the roads o... black motorbikes. In towns the municipal police handle traffic contro... If you are fined for a traffic offence, you will have to pay on the spo...

Rules and regulations. Always carry your driving licence wit... you. It is also a good idea to have a photocopy of the importan... pages of your passport with you.

Seat belts are compulsory. Children under 10 must travel in the rea...

Road signs. Apart from the standard international pictographs yo... may encounter the following:

Aparcamiento	Parking
Desviación	Detour
Obras	Road works
Peatones	Pedestrians
Peligro	Danger
Salida de camione	Truck exit
Senso unico	One way

¿Se puede aparcar aqui?	Can I park here?
Llénelo, por favor, con super.	Fill the tank please, top grade.
Ha habido un accidente.	There has been an accident.

E

ELECTRICITY *(corriente eléctrica)*

The standard supply is 220v with continental-style two-pin sockets... North American 110v appliances will need a transformer.

EMBASSIES AND CONSULATES *(consulados)*

Santa Cruz de Tenerife: **United Kingdom**: Plaza Weyler, 8, 1st Floor; tel: 922 286 863; fax: 922 289 903; open Mon–Fri 8am–2pm. **Republic of Eire**: Calle Castillo, 8, Fourth Floor A, 38002; tel: 922 245 671; fax: 922 249 957; open Mon–Fri 9am–1pm.

The nearest **United States** consulate is in Las Palmas, capital of the neighbouring Gran Canaria island, at Edificio Arca, Calle Los Martinez de Escobar 3, Oficina 7, tel: 928 271 259. It opens 10am–1pm weekdays. For other countries' representations, you may have to call Madrid.

If you lose your passport, or run into trouble with the authorities or the police, contact your consulate for advice. Consulates can issue temporary passports for a fee. You will need a statement of loss or theft from the police, plus two passport size photographs.

Where is the American/ British consulate?	**¿Dónde está el consulado americano/británico?**

EMERGENCIES *(urgencia)*

The general emergency number is 112. For police, fire brigade and 24-hour ambulance, call 922 532112.

Police	**Policía**
Fire	**Fuego**
Help!	**¡Socorro!**
Stop!	**¡Deténgase!**

Santa Cruz: University Hospital (tel: 922 790 401); Candelaria (tel: 922 766 362); Rambla (tel: 922 790 505).
Puerto de la Cruz: Bellevue (tel: 922 791 417); Tamaragua (tel: 922 380 512).
Las Americas: Hospital Las Americas (tel: 922 750 022).

Private hospitals accepting medical insurance *(see Health)* and running a free-phone 24-hour emergency service are: Hospiten Rambla, Santa Cruz (tel: 900 200 144); Hospiten Norte, Puerta de la Cruz (tel: 900 200 145); and Hospiten Sur, Playa de las Américas (tel: 900 200 143).

G

GAY AND LESBIAN TRAVELLERS

Major resorts in the Canary Islands have developed facilities for gay and lesbian travellers, including dedicated hotels. Check the website <www.gayinspain.com/canarias>.

GETTING TO TENERIFE

By air: There are numerous scheduled and cheap flights from all UK airports to Tenerife. The flight time is 4–4½ hours, and the cost around £150–350. Check the web and the travel sections of weekend newspapers. All-in package holidays can be the least expensive way to go. British Airways (tel: 0870 850 9850; <www.britishairways. com> and the national carrier Iberia (tel: 0845 850 9000; <www. iberia.com>) in the UK, also have promotional deals.

There are no direct flights to Tenerife from the US. Airlines go via major European airports, with the Spanish state airline Iberia (tel: 1-800 772-4642) going via Madrid, from where internal flights connect to all the Canary Islands. Flights can take 12–13 hours and cost around $1,000.

By ship: Trasmediterránea (<www.trasmediterranea.es>) has a limited number of sailings from Cádiz. For further details contact in the UK: Southern Ferries, 179 Piccadilly, London W1V 9DB (tel: 020 7491 4968); in Spain: Compañía Trasmediterránea, Alcalá, 61, 28014 Madrid (tel: 91 423 85 00); on Tenerife: Compañía Trasmediterránea, Estación Marítimo Muelle Ribera, Santa Cruz de Tenerife (fax only: 922 842 244).

GUIDES AND TOURS

The island is comprehensively covered by tour operators, whose coaches take tourists anywhere and everywhere that is worth seeing, both day and night. Check with the local tourist office, or at your hotel.

H

HEALTH & MEDICAL CARE

Non-EU visitors should have private medical insurance, and although there are reciprocal arrangements between EU countries, it is advisable for Britons to take out private insurance, too. The necessary E111 form is available at post offices in the UK. Make a photocopy that you can leave with the hospital or doctor. Before being treated, or before calling an ambulance, it is essential to establish that the doctor or service is working within the Spanish Health Service, otherwise you need to go elsewhere.

Dental treatment is not generally available under this system, so private insurance is strongly advised.

Farmácias (chemists/drugstores) can deal with a number of problems, and recommend remedies. They are usually open during normal shopping hours. After hours, at least one per town remains open all night. Called a *farmácia de guardia*, its location is posted in the window of all other *farmácias* nearby and printed in the local newspapers.

Where's the nearest (all-night) chemist?	**¿Dónde está la farmácia (de guardia) más cercana?**
I need a doctor/dentist.	**Necesito un médico/dentista.**
Sunburn/sunstroke	**quemadura del sol/una insolación**
An upset stomach	**molestias de estómago**
Is this service public or private?	**¿Es este servicio público o privado?**

HOLIDAYS *(día de fiesta)*

In addition to these Spanish national holidays, many purely local and lesser religious, civic and other holidays are celebrated in various towns of the archipelago *(see page 95)*.

1 January	*Año Nuevo*	New Year's Day
6 January	*Epifanía*	Epiphany
1 May	*Día del Trabajo*	Labour Day
15 August	*Asunción/Nuestra Señora de la Candelaria*	Assumption
12 October	*Día de la Hispanidad*	Discovery of America Day (Columbus Day)
1 November	*Todos los Santos*	All Saints' Day
6 December	*Día de la Constitución*	Constitution Day
8 December	*Inmaculada Concepción*	Immaculate Conception
25 December	*Navidad*	Christmas Day

Movable dates:

Carnaval	The week of Shrove Tuesday
Jueves Santo	Maundy Thursday
Viernes Santo	Good Friday
Corpus Christi	Corpus Christi

L

LANGUAGE

The Spanish spoken in the Canary Islands is a little different from that of the mainland. For instance, islanders don't lisp when they pronounce the letters c or z. The language of the Canaries is spoken with a slight lilt, reminiscent of the Caribbean, and a number of New World words and expressions are used. The most common

Do you speak English?	**¿Habla usted inglés?**
I don't speak Spanish.	**No hablo español.**

re *guagua* (pronounced wah-wah), meaning bus, and *papa* (pota-o). In tourist areas German, English and some French is often spo-en, or at least understood.

The *Berlitz Spanish Phrasebook and Dictionary* covers most sit-ations you may encounter in your travels in Spain and the Canaries.

LOST PROPERTY *(Objetos perdidos)*

The first thing to do when you discover you have lost something is obviously to retrace your steps. If you still cannot find the missing tem, report the loss to the Municipal Police or the Guardia Civil *(see Police)*.

I've lost my wallet/ pocketbook/passport.	**He perdido mi cartera/bolso/ pasaporte.**

M

MAPS

Maps are generally available, though walking maps are less easy to come by, and should be purchased if possible before going to the area you plan to walk.

MEDIA

Radio and television *(radio; televisión)*: Many hotels have satel-lite television with several stations in many languages. The larger islands all include some English-language news and tourist infor-mation in their programming. English-language radio stations on Tenerife include Radio FM 95.3 MHz; Power FM 91.2 MHz; Waves FM 96.8 MHz.

Newspapers and periodicals: Many major British and continental papers are on sale in the Canaries on the day of publication. There are a number of English-language publications with Canarian news and tourist information, which are not very evenly distributed. These include *Tenerife News*, a fortnightly paper, also available on the web (<www.tennews.com>), the monthly *Living Tenerife* and the on-line *News Canaries* (<www.ic-web.com>) as well as various property-based publications.

There is also a good annual restaurant guide, *¡Qué Bueno!* in English and Spanish.

MONEY MATTERS

Currency: The monetary unit in the Canary Islands, as throughout Spain, is the euro, symbolised €. Bank notes are available in denominations of 500, 200, 100, 50, 20, 10 and 5. The euro is sub divided into 100 cents and there are coins available for €1 and €2 and for 50, 20, 10, 5, 2 and 1 cent.

Currency exchange. Banks are the best place to exchange currency. *Casas de cambio* stay open outside banking hours, as do some other businesses displaying a *cambio* sign. All larger hotels will also change guests' money, but the rate is slightly less favourable than at the bank. Both banks and exchange offices pay slightly less for cash than for travellers' cheques. Always take your passport when you go to change money.

Credit cards. Major cards are widely recognised on Tenerife, although smaller businesses still tend to prefer cash. Visa, Eurocard/MasterCard are the cards that are most generally accepted. Credit and debit cards are also useful for obtaining cash from ATMs – cash machines – which are to be found in all towns and resorts. They offer the most convenient way of obtaining cash and will usually give you the best exchange rate.

Travellers' cheques. Hotels, shops, restaurants and travel agencies all cash travellers' cheques, and so do banks, where you are likely to get a better rate (you will need to show your passport). It is safest to cash small amounts at any one time, thereby retaining some of your holiday funds in cheques, which you can keep in the hotel

afe. Banking hours are usually from 9am–2pm Monday to Friday,
nd on public holidays (see Holidays).

Where's the nearest bank (currency exchange office)?	**¿Dónde está el banco (la oficina de cambio) más cercana?**
I want to change some dollars/pounds.	**Quiero cambiar dólares/ Libres esterlina.**
Do you accept travellers' checks?	**¿Acepta usted cheques de viajero?**
Can I pay with this credit card?	**¿Puedo pagar con esta tarjeta de crédito?**

O

OPENING HOURS

Shops, offices and other businesses generally observe the afternoon
iesta, opening from Monday to Saturday 9am–1pm and 4–8pm
some on Saturday morning only). In tourist areas many places
lon't open until 10am, but they then stay open all day. Post offices
re open from 9am–2pm.

Most commercial premises are closed on Sunday even in the
nost commercialised resorts.

P

POLICE *(policía)*

There are three police forces in Tenerife, as in the rest of Spain.
The *Guardia Civil* (Civil Guard) is the main force. Each town also
as its own *Policía Municipal* (municipal police), whose uniform
varies depending on the town and season but is mostly blue and
grey. The third force, the *Cuerpo Nacional de Policía*, is a national anti-crime unit that wears a light-brown uniform. All police offi-

cers are armed. Spanish policing is strict but officers are generally
courteous to foreign visitors.

Where is the nearest police station?	**¿Dónde está la comisaría más cercana?**

POST OFFICES *(correos)*

Post offices are for mail and telegrams, not telephone calls. Stamps
(sellos) are sold at any tobacconist's *(estancos)* and by most shops
selling postcards. See the web site, <www.correos.es>.

Mailboxes are painted yellow. If one of the slots is marked
extranjero, it means it is for letters abroad.

Where is the (nearest) post office?	**¿Dónde está la oficina de correos (más cercana)?**
A stamp for this letter/ postcard, please.	**Por favor, un sello para esta carta/tarjeta.**

PUBLIC TRANSPORT

Airlines: A number of airlines operate flights between the islands
which are not much more expensive than ferries. Binter Canarias
(tel: 922 630 184; <www.bintercanarias.es>), a privatised sub-
sidiary of Iberia, has the most flights. Spanair (tel: 902 131 415
<www.spanair.com>), also has flights.
Bus services: Buses *(guaguas)* are frequent, fast and cheap, with
tickets purchased on board and change given. TITSA (Transporte
Interurbanos de Tenerife SA) runs efficient services around the
island and timetables can be found at bus depots, tourist office or
call 922 531 300 <www.titsa.com>. There are no trains.
Ferry services: Trasmediterránea (tel: 902 454 654) runs ferries to
Gran Canaria, taking four hours for the 63-km (39-mile) crossing

The Fred Olsen jetfoil takes 80 minutes to Agaete, where there is a free connecting bus to Las Palmas, taking another hour. Fred Olsen Lines also serves neighbouring La Gomera and Hierro from Los Cristianos. Further information from Fred Olsen SA, Dr Zerolo 14, Santa Cruz de Tenerife (tel: 902 100 107). Note that if you have bought your ticket in advance, it must be confirmed at the desk half an hour before departure.

R

RELIGION

The predominant religion of Tenerife is Catholicism, which is deeply observed. The Madonna of Candelaria is the patron saint of the whole of the Canaries, bringing pilgrims from all of Spain. On Tenerife the bishop's see is in La Laguna. Tourists should respect local sensibilites and not enter churches dressed for the beach, or intrude on public and private prayer.

T

TAXES

Impuestos Generalisado Indirecto Canario (IGIC) is levied on all goods and services at a rate of 5 percent.

TAXIS

The letters SP *(servicio público)* on the front and rear bumpers of a car indicate that it is a taxi; it might also have a green light in the front windscreen or a green sign indicating '*libre*' when it is free. Fixed prices are displayed on a board at the main taxi rank, giving

| How much is it to Hotel Mencey/the town centre? | **¿Cuanto es al Hotel Mencey/ al centro?** |

the fares to the most popular destinations. These are reasonable and in general taxis, which are easily found in urban areas, provide an inexpensive method of transport. If in doubt, just ask the driver before setting off.

TELEPHONES *(teléfono)*

Phone booths *(kioskos)* accept coins and cards *(tarjetas telefónicas)* available from tobacconists. Instructions in English, along with area codes for different countries, are displayed clearly. International calls are expensive, so be sure to have a plentiful supply of coins or enough money on your card. For international direct dialling, wait for the dial tone, then dial 00, wait for a second tone and dial the country code, area code (minus the initial zero) and number. In some places there are *cabinas*, phone cabins where you make your call and pay afterwards.

For American visitors, calling directly from your hotel room is expensive unless you are using a calling card, or some other similar system, from a long-distance supplier such as AT&T or MCI. Find out from the supplier which free connection number is applicable to Spain (they are different for each country) before you leave, as these numbers are not always easily available once there.

Check before leaving home to see if your mobile phones will operate from the Canary Islands, and within Tenerife. The local mobile phone system is called Star and it is used by oversees providers.

Operator: The number for the international operator is 025.

Country codes: For the US and Canada dial 1, Great Britain 44, Australia 61, New Zealand 64, the Republic of Ireland 353 and South Africa 27.

Local codes: The code for Spain in +34. For the Canary Islands a prefix must always be dialled, even for local calls: Province of Santa Cruz de Tenerife (Tenerife, El Hierro, La Gomera and La Palma) 922; Province of Las Palmas de Gran Canaria (Gran Canaria, Lanzarote and Fuerteventura) 928.

TIME DIFFERENCES

n winter the Canaries maintain Greenwich Mean Time, which is one hour behind most European countries, including Spain, but the same as the UK. For the rest of the year the islands go on summer time, as does Spain – keeping the one-hour difference.
Winter time chart:

Los Angeles	New York	London	**Canaries**	Madrid
4am	7am	noon	**noon**	1pm

TIPPING *(propinas)*

Since a service charge is often included in restaurant bills, tipping is not obligatory. Ten percent of the bill is usual for taxi drivers, bar staff, waiters and hairdressers. Also tip porters and maids a few euros, depending on length of stay.

TOILETS

The most commonly used expressions for toilets in the Canaries are *servicios* or *aseos*, though you may also hear or see WC *(doobla-vay say)* and *retretes*.

Public conveniences are rare, but most hotels, bars and restaurants have lavatories. It is considered polite to buy a coffee if you do drop into a bar to use their facilities.

Where are the lavatories? **¿Dónde están los servicios?**

TOURIST INFORMATION

Information on the Canary Islands may be obtained from <www.spain.info> or from Spanish National Tourist Offices:
Australia: International House, Suite 44, 104 Bathurst Street, PO Box A-675, 2000 Sydney NSW, tel: 02-264 79 66.

Canada: 2 Bloor Street West, 34th Floor, Toronto, Ontario M4V
3E2; tel: (416) 961-3131, fax: (416) 961-1992, e-mail: spainto@
globalserve.net.
UK: 22–3 Manchester Square, London, W1U 3PX; tel: 020 748(
8077 (visits by appointment); e-mail: tourspain@latestinfo.co.uk
brochure line, tel: 08459 400180 (Republic of Ireland 0818 220290)
US: Chicago: Water Tower Place, Suite 915 East, 845 Nortl
Michigan Avenue, Chicago, IL 60611; tel: (312) 642-1992, fax: (312
642-9817, e-mail: buzon.oficial@chicago.oet.mcx.es.
Los Angeles: 8383 Wilshire Boulevard, Suite 960, Beverly Hills
Los Angeles, CA 90211; tel: (213) 658 7188, fax: (323) 658-1061
e-mail: buzon.oficial@losangeles.oet.mcx.es.
New York: 665 Fifth Avenue, New York, NY 10103; tel: (212) 265
8822, fax: (212) 265-8864, e-mail: buzon.oficial@nuevayork
oet.mcx.es.
Miami: 1221 Brickell Avenue, Miami, Florida, FL 33131; tel: (305
358-1992, fax: (305) 358-8223, e-mail: buzon.oficial@miami
oet.mcx.es.

In **Tenerife**, the main office for the whole island is the Cabildo
Insular in Plaza de España; tel: 922 239 592, fax: 239 812
<www.cabtfe.es> (in Spanish); open Mon–Fri 8am–6pm, Sa
9am–1pm.

Information may also be obtained from local offices:
Adeje: Avenida Rafael Puig, 1 (by the Playa de Troya); tel/fax: 922
750 633; open Mon–Fri 9am–2.30pm.
Aeropuerto Tenerife-Sur Reina Sofia (Arrivals Terminal)
tel: 922 392 037; open Mon–Fri 9am–9pm, Sat 9am–1pm.
Candelaria/Las Caletillas: Avenida del Generalisimo, s/n; tel: 922
500 415.
El Médano: Plaza de los Principes de España; tel: 922 176 002; oper
Mon–Fri (summer) 9am–2pm, (winter) 9am–3pm and Sat 9am–1pm
La Laguna: Plaza del Adelantado; tel: 922 631 194; open Mon–Sa
8am–8pm.

La Oratova: Calle Carrera del Escultor Estevez, 2; tel: 922 323 041, fax: 922 323 142; open Mon–Fri 9am–6pm.

Las Galletas: Avenida Maritima; tel: 922 730 133; open Mon–Fri 9am–3.30pm, Sat 9am–1pm.

Los Cristianos: Centro Cultural (Casa de La Cultura, opposite the Mobil fuel station), Calle General Franco, s/n; tel: 922 757 137, fax: 752 492; open Mon–Fri 9am–3.30pm, Sat 9am–1pm.

Playa de Las Américas, Arona: Centro Comercial; tel: 922 797 068, fax: 922 757 198; open Mon–Fri 9am–9pm, Sat 9am–5pm.

Playa de Las Vistas: Paseo Maritimo, tel: 922 787 011, e-mail: vistas@atlantis.es; open Mon–Fri 9am–5pm.

Puerto de La Cruz: Plaza de Europa, s/n; tel: 922 386 000, fax 384 769; open Mon–Fri 9am–8pm (9am–7pm July–Sept) and Sat 9am–1pm.

Santa Cruz de Tenerife: Cabildo Insular (Plaza de Espana); tel: 922 239 592, fax: 239 812; open Mon–Fri 8am–6pm, Sat 9am–1pm.

Santiago del Teide: Centro Commercial 'Seguro el Sol' (near the Playa de la Arena), Calle Manuel Ravelo, 20–Local 35; tel/fax: 922 860 348; open Mon–Fri 9.30am–3.30pm, Sat 9.30am–12.30pm.

TRAVELLERS WITH DISABILITIES

Tenerife's climate makes it favourite place for recuperation, and it is well adapted to the needs of travellers with disabilities. There are wheelchair ramps at the major airports and many larger apartments and hotels make provision for disabled guests. Some of the more modern resorts also provide ramps to cross pavements. The facilities at Los Cristianos are renowned among disabled travellers and the Marisol Resort in particular specialises in holidays for such guests and their families. Access Travel in the United Kingdom (tel: 01942 888844) is one operator that goes there. Wheelchairs can be hired from Ortopedia Hospitalaria Lero, Puerto De La Cruz (tel: 922 750 289, fax: 922 750 283).

W

WATER *(agua)*

Tap water is safe to drink but can have a tang to it, so people gen
erally prefer to drink bottled water: *con gas* (sparkling) and *sin ga*
(still). Remember that water is scarce, so don't waste it.

WEBSITES

There are internet cafés in Santa Cruz, Puerto de la Cruz, Lo
Cristianos and Playa de las Américas. Libraries have internet facil
ities, but you cannot use them for emails.

There a number of websites with useful up-to-date informatio
about Tenerife. The following is just a selection:

- <www.canary-live.com> (up-to-date information on events)
- <www.canarysearch.net> (search engine for the Canary Islands)
- <www.ecoturismo.canarios.com> (rural tourism accommodation
- <www.puntoinfo.idecnet.com> (island tourist office official site)
- <www.tennews.com> (local fortnightly paper on-line)
- <www.thinkspain.com> (regional news of Spain)
- <www.spaintour.com/canarias> (Spanish tourist office website)

Recommended Hotels

This selection of hotels is designed to give a cross section of accommodation available in the main towns *(for details of accommodation in general, see page 106)*. It's best to book in advance, particularly in high season or at carnival time, when prices go up. High season is November to February, July and August. Don't expect to find accommodation everywhere — it is mainly concentrated in the larger towns and resorts. As a basic guide to room prices we have used the following symbols for a double room with bath/shower in high season:

€€€€ €120-plus
€€€ €80–120
€€ €40–80
€ under €40

THE NORTHEAST

ANAGA

Albergue Montes de Anaga € *tel: 922 822 056; fax: 922 310 793; <www.alberguestenerife.net>.* This modern, three-storey block with 9 bedrooms (sleeping between 2 and 6 people) is just about the only place to stay in the middle of the Parque Rural de Anaga. Fabulously set in a remote location, with impressive views, it is walker-friendly, and you can also hire bikes here and get information about the park. Breakfast is provided.

LA LAGUNA

Aguere €€ *Calle La Carrera 55, tel: 922 259 490; fax: 922 631 533.* This mansion in the middle of the World Heritage quarter of town was at one time the home of the bishop of Tenerife. It became a hotel in 1885 and passed into the present family's hands in 1920.

There are 22 en-suite bedrooms and its facilities only merit on star, hence its wonderful value.

Nivaria €€€ *Plaza del Adelantado 11, tel: 922 264 298; fax 922 259 634*. This apartment-hotel is in the main square in th centre of the old town. Based on an 18th-century mansion, it ha a new block behind. Apartments are spacious, with cooking facil ities, and cost no more than a regular mid-priced hotel. Som parking available.

Pensión Berlin € *Calle República de Venezuela 62, tel: 922 25. 043*. There are two *pensiónes* in this university and UNESCO Worl Heritage town, which is short on accommodation. This one is jus outside the old town and should be booked in advance.

SANTA CRUZ

Anaga €€ *Imeldo Serís 19, tel: 922 245 090; fax: 922 245 644* This modern block by the old town is utilitarian, but it is conve niently situated within walking distance of the ferry and pedestri anised shopping streets. It's also inexpensive, and there is a grea view of the town from the roof.

Atlántico €€ *Castillo 12, tel: 922 246 375; fax: 922 246 378. A* cheerful, central, two-star hotel with a restaurant at street level, thi is part of a trio of hotels: the one-star Océanic *(tel: 922 270 800 fax: 922 270 089)* is at No. 6 and the El Dorado *(tel: 922 243 184 fax: 922 243 259)* at Cruz Verde 24. All are within a few metres o each other, have TV and offer breakfast. Perfectly acceptable mid price accommodation.

Pensión Casa Blanca € *Calle Viera y Clavijo 15; tel: 922 27 599*. One of half a dozen *pensiónes* in the town, and reasonabl central. Some rooms have balconies, though none have en-suit baths, but it's a clean, cheerful, friendly place.

Plaza €€€ *Plaza de la Candelaria 9, tel: 922 246 862; fax: 92 247 278*. Efficiently run and situated right in the heart of the pedes rian shopping streets by the port, this 95-room hotel suited for business as well as leisure and has rooms with disabled access.

Sheraton Mencey €€€€ *Doctor José Navéiras 38, tel: 922 609 000; fax: 922 280 017; <www.luxurycollection.com/mencey>*. Old-fashioned luxury in the heart of town, close to the parliament, and used by government officials and visiting dignitaries. There are tennis courts, casino, swimming pool and a top-notch restaurant.

THE NORTH

EL TEIDE

Parador de Cañadas del Teide €€€€ *38300 La Orotava, tel: 922 386 415; fax: 922 382 352; <paradores-spain.es>*. The only *parador* (state-run hotel) on the island has a stunning setting directly under El Teide, next to the unusual peaks of Los Roques and close to the cable car, and is decorated in Canary Islands style. It's worth dropping in for a coffee or meal if you are not staying. Guests can watch the sun rise over the volcano and beat the cable-car crowds. It has a pool, sauna and gymnasium. Best to opt for half board. 23 rooms.

LA OROTAVA

Pensión Silene € *Tomas Zerolo 9, tel/fax: 922 330 199*. Feel at home in this elegant *pensión* in a 19th-century town house.

Victoria €€€ *Hermano Apolinar 8, tel: 922 331 683; fax: 922 320 519*. A handsome 18th-century mansion with an internal courtyard in the old quarter, and 13 double en-suite rooms. The pleasant restaurant has good local dishes and wines. There is a fine view of both the town and El Teide from the roof terrace.

LOS REALEJOS

Maritim Tenerife €€€ *El Burgado 1, tel: 922 379 000; fax: 922 379 027*. This four-star, high-rise hotel is set in a tropical garden on the rocky coast, just outside Puerto de la Cruz, and has a sparkling

outdoor pool and terrace overlooking the sea. Rooms are function
al, with good views. Entertainment is laid on and there is a free bus
into town 15 minutes' ride away.

PUERTO DE LA CRUZ

Atalaya Gran Hotel €€€ *Parque Taoro, tel: 922 384 451; fax
922 387 046.* Traditional family style hotel with stunning views
over the town and coast, and set in its own huge tropical garden
Some rooms are wheelchair accessible. Large heated pool, sporting
opportunities and free entry to the casino. 183 rooms.

Los Genarios € *Calle Lomo, tel: 922 382 810; fax: 922 382 810*
A clean and pleasant *pensión* in a quiet street in the old part of town

Hotel Botánico and Oriental Spa Garden €€€€ *Avenida
Richard J. Yeoward, 1, tel: 922 381 400; fax: 922 381 504; <www.
hotelbotanico.com>.* Set in 2.5 hectares (6 acres) of gardens and
parklands, this top, five-star luxury hotel has an elegant and peace-
ful atmosphere with views over the ocean and Mt Teide. Four
restaurants, bars, boutiques and a health centre. 251 rooms.

Hotel Chimisay €€ *Agustín Bethencourt 14, tel: 922 383 552,
fax: 922 382 840; <www.hotel-chimisay.com>.* A modern, small
mid-price hotel in a pedestrianised street a few minutes from Plaza
del Charco. It has 63 rooms, some with balconies, a swimming pool
sauna and massage parlour.

Hotel-Residencia Regulo €€ *Calle Pérez Zamora, 16, tel: 922
384 506; fax 922 370 420.* A small, friendly hotel near the Plaza del
Charco, with 14 rooms and a rooftop terrace to catch the sun.

Marquesa €€€ *Quintana 11, tel: 922 383 151; fax: 922 386 950,
<www.hotelmarquesa.com>.* One of the most beautiful mansions
in town, built in 1712, has been extended to provide 144 rooms
most with balconies. The terrace at the front of the hotel overlooks
the pedestrianised street and is ideal for people-watching. There is
a swimming pool and sauna.

Monopol €€€ *Quintana 15, tel: 922 384 611; fax: 922 370 310.* Next door but one to the Marquesa *(see above)*, this is an equally handsome mansion and its lovely balconied courtyard makes an elegant lobby. There are 92 rooms with all amenities, swimming pool and sauna.

Puerto Azul €€ *Lomo 24, tel/fax: 922 383 213.* A pleasant, small, modern, two-star hotel just off the central Plaza del Charco. Eight of the 26 basic rooms are singles and two have large terraces. The roof terrace is open to all guests.

San Telmo €€ *Calle San Telmo 18, tel: 922 385 853; fax: 922 385 991.* Right on the seafront, with balconied rooms overlooking the sea (for just a few euros more), which splashes against the rocks all night long. Not posh, this is a delightful, old-fashioned hotel, with a breezy seaside feel. Breakfast is included in the price and there's a rooftop pool.

THE NORTHWEST

GARACHICO

Hotel Rural El Patio €€ *Finca Malpais, El Guincho, tel 922 133 280; fax: 922 830 089; <www.hotelpatio.com>.* Inland and just east of Garachico, the hotel is on a banana plantation in a house that is said to date from the 16th century. There are 26 bedrooms in three units decorated in rural style. Walks head off through the gardens and plantations and there is a heated pool and restaurant.

Pensión El Jardín € *Esteban de Ponte 4, tel: 922 830 245.* This delightful family-run *pensión* is in an old townhouse with patio. The bedrooms leading off the first-floor landing have no windows, but are spacious and comfortable with original furniture. There is a large family attic room with rooftop views. The hotel can also organise diving trips.

La Quinta Roja €€€ *Glorieta de San Francisco s/n, tel: 922 133 377; fax: 922 133 360; <www.quintaroja.com>.* This lovely mansion in the quiet central square is a survivor of the 18th century earthquake. It was home of the Marqués of Quinta Roja and is typical of island baroque style. Opened in 2002, it is very much plugged into local activities, organising excursions into the countryside. Don't miss the turtles in the outside pool.

THE SOUTH

GRANADILLA DE ABONA

Hotel Rural Senderos de Abona €€ *Calle Peatonal de la Iglesia 5, tel: 922 770 200; fax: 922 770 308.* An enclosed hotel that was once the post office, in the quiet streets of Garanadilla. The rooms are in period and there is a good restaurant as well as a collection of tools and implements in a 'museum'. Only the clock on the church opposite disturbs the peace, every quarter of an hour.

EL MÉDANO

Hotel Médano €€€ *La Playa del Médano s/n, tel: 922 177 000; fax: 922 176 048; <www.medano.es>.* On the beach with four sun terraces, overlooking the sea and the Montaña Roja. Offers wind surfing, kitesurfing, scuba diving, trekking, cycling and golf.

Playa Sur Tenerife €€ *E-38612 El Medano, tel: 922 176 120; fax: 922 176 337; <www.hotelplayasurtenerife.es>.* Isolated in the middle of a long stretch of beach, this has long been a windsurfers' choice, with boards for hire. It faces the beach on either side so all rooms have balconies with views. There is a pool and bar.

GÜÍMAR

Casona Santo Domingo €€ *Calle Santa Domingo 32, tel: 922 510 229; fax: 922 514 451.* An elegant, central *hotel rural* dating from the 16th century, with pitch pine balconies, period furniture and a common sitting room with coffee-table books about the area. The restaurant serves a menu of local dishes. Dogs and chicken will guard your car in the yard.

Hotel Rural Finca Salamanca €€ *Carretera Güimar–El Puertito, Km1.5, tel: 922 514 530; fax: 922 514 061; <www.hotel-fincasalamanca.com>*. A manor house, in a country estate, that has been converted into a charming small hotel for those who want peace and quiet and still enjoy top class facilities. 16 rooms.

THE SOUTHWEST

ADEJE

Fonda Central €€ *Carrer Grande 6, tel: 922 781 550*. An attractive noble house, with courtyard, dating from the 18th century, situated in the old part of town; the hotel has three rooms en suite, a solarium, bar and restaurant.

LOS CRISTIANOS

Arona Gran Hotel €€ *Avenida de Cristianos, tel: 922 750 678; fax: 922 750 243*. On the beach at the end of Los Cristianos harbour, all rooms are modern and have a terrace overlooking the water. Sports facilities, restaurants and bars, and a wonderful atrium lobby bedecked with green plants hanging from each floor. Good value. 400 rooms.

Hotel Andrea €€ *Avenida del Valle Menendez, tel: 922 7 90 012; fax: 922 794 270*. One of the few non four-star hotels in Los Cristianos, this is a modern block that's easy to find as you come into town. Try to get a room overlooking the street as inner rooms are a bit gloomy. No breakfast, but connected to a downstairs pizza restaurant.

La Paloma € *San Juan XXIII, tel: 922 790 198*. One of half a dozen *pensiónes* around the old part of town. The full-blown restaurant downstairs is one of the better pavement places to eat in town.

PLAYA DE LAS AMÉRICAS

Flamingo Suites €€€€ *Avenida España s/n, Playa de las Américas, tel: 922 718 400; fax: 922 718 401; <www.flamingo-*

tenerife.com>. These luxury apartments in the heart of Playa de las Américas are considered Tenerife's most exclusive private club. Every modern facility, including Jacuzzi tubs, plunge pools and daily maid service. 18 suites.

Gran Tacande €€€ *Calle Walter Paetzman s/n, tel: 922 746 400; fax: 922 746 377.* One of the Dreamplace resorts that tries to look like a swanky village, built in various Canarian architectural styles. By the sea with heated salt-water pool. There are 207 rooms, plus the Royal or Imperial suites with their own Jacuzzi, reception and lounges.

Mare Nostrum Resort €€€€ *Avenda de las Américas s/n, tel: 922 757 500; fax: 922 753 226.* Fantasy classical land in one of five 5-star hotels – Sir Anthony, Cleopatra, Julio Cesar, Marco Antonio and Mediterranean Palace (with rooftop nudist zone and pool). Together they provide more than a thousand rooms, 102 with their own private pools, with thalassotherapy a speciality, and 13 restaurants. You won't even know you are in Tenerife.

VILAFLOR

Alta Montaña € *Alta Montaña Morro el Cano 5, tel: 922 709 049.* An inexpensive stop on the top of the world, this is one of three *pensiónes* in Vilaflor.

Hotel de Alta Montaña €€ *Carretera San Roque s/n, tel 922 709 341.* 'The highest hotel in Spain' is the boast of this modern hotel 1,660m (5,450ft) above sea level. There are 22 spacious rooms with all facilities including DVDs, gym and Jacuzzi. All kinds of activities in the area are available through the hotel, including hang-gliding, mountain biking and climbing.

El Nogal €€ *Camino Real s/n La Escalona, tel: 922 726 050; fax: 922 725 853.* Half way to heaven, this secluded 19th-century estate between Arona and Vilaflor has been converted into a hotel by its owners, descendants of the orginal Linares family. There are 40 double rooms tastefully furnished.

Recommended Restaurants

Listed below is a pot pouri of restaurants to be found around the island. They have been chosen because of their originality, setting, convenience or simply for the quality of their food. *Tinerfeños* eat late by northern European standards, starting lunch around 2 or 3pm, and dinner around 9 or 10pm.

Eating is not expensive on the island. Fixed-price menus *(menú del día)*, generally available at lunchtime only, can be as little as €7 for three courses and a glass of wine. To give you an idea of price (for two; a three-course meal including a bottle of house wine), we have used the following symbols:

€€€€	over €80
€€€	€50–80
€€	€20–50
€	under €20

THE NORTHEAST

ANAGA

Cruz del Carmen €€ *Las Mercedes Km6, tel: 922 250 062*. An ideal stop, by the Cruz del Carmen *mirador*, when exploring the Anaga Hills. Good solid Canarian cooking, with both meat and fish soups and home-made sweets, in three spacious dining rooms. There's a bar here, too.

LA LAGUNA

Casa Maquila €€ *Callejón de Maquile s/n, tel: 922 257 020*. This is a reliable local, with several individual rooms and regulars who chat at the bar. Parrot fish and squid are on the menu, together with chickpea staples, and simple dishes of mushrooms, peas and ham. Look out for the Tacoronte on the wine list.

Las Cazuelitas del Marqués €€€ *Carre Herradores 105, tel: 922 251 975*. An intimate, friendly place with a busy domestic interior. Locals pop in for a drink and chat with the chef-owner, Adolfo González and his wife, Aida. Portions are generous and the menu is innovative.

La Posada de los Mosqueteros €€ *Calle Sant Domongo 4, tel: 922 254 965*. A *tasca* known for its selection of hams and cheeses, and local dishes such as pheasant and rabbit with prawns.

LOS NARANJEROS

Restaurant La Bara €€ *Carretera General del Norte Km398, tel: 922 563 820*. The house specialities are soups made with local wines. Other soups are conjured up from boiled salted fish. Roast meats are also in plentiful supply.

La Vara €€ *Carretera del Norte*. Set in an old house with a number of dining rooms, this is one of many popular meat restaurants, between La Laguna and Tacoronte, which fill up at weekend lunchtimes.

SANTA CRUZ

El Aguila €€ *Plaza Alféreces Provis, tel: 922 273 156*. In a central pedestrian square with lots to watch – including a large screen outside when a big football game is on. Has an extensive selection of *tapas* with large *parillas* of fish or meat – go to the counter and point to the ones that take your fancy.

Bodega San Sebastián €€ *Avenida San Sebastián 55, tel: 922 216 853*. One of the oldest *bodegas* in the town, with scores of wines to choose from.

Café del Principe €€ *Plaza del Principe del Asturias, tel: 922 278 810*. This iron-and-glass art nouveau pavilion in a shady town square is an enjoyable place for either *tapas* of such local dishes as *pulpo con mojo*, or for a full meal.

El Corte Inglés €€€€ *Avenida 3 de Mayo, tel: 922 849 400.* The top-floor restaurant of the famous department store has a cool modern design, with a large expanse of windows giving one of the best views over Santa Cruz. The menu changes regularly and is an eclectic mix of seafood and meat dishes.

El Coto del Antonio €€ *Calle General Goded 13, tel: 922 272 105.* An intimate *tasca*-like restaurant off the Rambla, serving Canarian and Basque food, such as baby bean salad with lobster, and goat in almond sauce.

La Hierbita € *Calle Clavel 19 , tel: 922 244617.* An old house with many small, well-decorated small rooms on two floors. Rabbit stew and other good local dishes. Try the *hierbita* liqueur made by the owner.

Tasca La Norta €€€ *Calle Calendaria 15, tel: 922 292 047.* This small *tasca* near the old town has innovative modern Canarian cuisine. There are no starters or main courses, but a selection of individual mid-price dishes, from liver on toast to Roquefort-stuffed salmon.

THE NORTH

EL SAUZAL

Casa del Vino La Baranda €€€ *Autopista General del Norte Km21, tel: 922 572 535.* The restaurant in this elegant 17th-century estate, now occupied by the wine museum, serves good modern Canarian food, and is the best place to try – and ask about – Canarian wines. There is also a *tasca* bar with views from the terrace down to the sea. Closed Mondays.

ICOD DE LOS VINOS

La Cueva de San Marcos €€ *Carretera del Amparo 97, tel: 922 812 442.* This *finca* located right in the middle of the wine-growing area makes and bottles 20,000 litres of its own red and white wine every year. The informal restaurant, with four terrace tables, offers excellent Canarian home-cooking.

LA OROTAVA

El Engazo €€ *Finca Taluriaste s/n, tel: 922 333 556.* The *finca* of the Pontes Mendéz estate was bought by the current chef Manuel Luis Dominguez in 1963, since when it has acquired a reputation for friendliness and good local dishes, such as spare ribs with corn on the cob. Closed Thursdays and Sunday evenings.

Sabor Canario €€ *Carrer Carrera 17, tel: 922 322 793.* When in La Orotava's historic centre, you need to eat in an old townhouse such as this, which dates from 1580. The dishes are traditional too, including rabbit in *solmerejo* sauce, and various manifestations of *gofio* (roasted barley flour). A good selection of wines.

PUERTO DE LA CRUZ

Bodegón Casa Antigua €€ *Carrer San Felipe 23, tel: 922 371 472.* A delightful old house in the fishermen's quarter, divided into small rooms, with lots of photos and memorabilia. Goat and tuna are usually on the menu.

Bodegón Las Palmeras € *Carrer Méquinez 45, tel: 922 382 907.* Budget meals are served in this check-cloth café in the fishermen's quarter. Fish or meat of the day are fresh and simply grilled.

Casa de Miranda €€ *Calle Santo Domingo, 13 (Plaza de Europa), Puerto de la Cruz, tel: 922 373 871.* This attractive Canarian mansion, with wooden beams, floors and staircases, dates from 1730. The *bodeguita* on the lower floor has a selection of hams and cheeses. The upstairs restaurant has fish and shellfish specialities.

Los Faroles €€ *Av. Francisco Afonso, tel: +34 922 384616.* The biggest barbecue on the island is famous for its traditional dishes and is a hit with locals as well as visitors.

La Gañaninía €€€ *Camino El Durazno s/n, tel: 922 371 000.* Up towards the motorway near the Abaco museum-house, this is the converted stable of an 18th-century farmhouse with wonderful views over Puerto de la Cruz. The menu is Canarian, with *tapas* dishes.

The Oriental €€€€ *Avenida Richard J. Yeoward, tel: 922 381 400.* Located within the Hotel Botánico, the speciality is Thai cookery with Pan-Asiatic touches. The ambiance here is formal (jacket and tie are obligatory) and the cuisine is enticing. Open for dinner every evening.

Régulo €€€ *Calle Pérez Zamora, 16, Puerto de la Cruz; tel: 922 384 506.* One of the best restaurants in town, situated in a typical Canarian 18th-century house with balconies around a delightful patio. Specialities include *lapas a la plancha* (grilled limpet shells) and *solomillo relleno de camembert* (fillet steak with camembert stuffing). Open for lunch and dinner, closed Sundays and all July.

TEGUESTE

Casa Tomás € *c/Camina del Portezuelo 2, tel: 922 638 007.* Homemade Canarian food, dishes including spare ribs with potatoes and chickpea stews. Busy at weekends.

El Drago €€€ *Carrer Marqués de Celada 2, tel: 922 543 001.* A restaurant worth looking out for, this award-winning establishment is run by Carlos Gamonal Jiménez and his sons. They serve some of the best Canarian dishes on the island, much of it their own creation, such as watercress soup with yam, red onion, cheese and *gofio*.

THE NORTHWEST

BUENAVISTA DEL NORTE

Rincón del Norte €€ *Avenida Juan Méndez el Viejo 10, tel: 922 127 301.* This restaurant serves international and local dishes, with daily variations, including *tapas*. The owner, José Méndez Baez, speaks English. Closed Wednesdays.

EL TANQUE

Mirador Lomo Molino €€ *Carretera Tierra del Trigo 22, tel: 922 136 680.* Fabulous views over Los Silos and Garachico. This is a teaching restaurant and it serves excellent, innovative food.

GARACHICO

Hotel San Roque €€€€ *Calle Esteban de Ponte 32, tel: 922 133 435.* Eat in a small dining room or at tables around the pool. The cuisine is as eclectic as the ambiance. Expect to find such delicacies as *daurade au sel* (fish baked in rock salt) and *paella duo* (made with vegetables and squid).

Isla Baja €€ *Esteban de Ponte 5, tel: 922 830 008.* An old town house with a cool courtyard and a model of the volcanic eruption that destroyed the town. Traditional local dishes.

MASCA

Restaurante-bar Mirador 'La Fuente' €€ *Bajada a la Plaza, tel: 922 863 466.* In the village just below the road and with marvellous views through the mountains, this place has local produce on sale, as well as basic Canarian dishes and delicious fruit drinks.

THE SOUTH

CHAYOFA

La Finca del Arte €€ *Calle del Centro 1, tel: 922 729 103.* Situated between Playa de las Américas and Arona, this former tomato packing factory is run by Wolfgang Eggar, and it functions as an art gallery for local talent as well as a café and bistro. Good to drop in to any time of day; it livens up on Sundays with a jazz brunch.

GRANADILLA DE ABONA

Bodega El jable €€ *Carrer Betenjuí 9, tel: 922 390 698.* Twice winner of the Best Canarian Cuisine award, this is where to find creative local dishes. Try the watercress soup or the tuna *(albacora)* with dry fruit vinaigrette.

GUIA DE ISIDORA

Casa Juana €€€ *Calle Virgen de la Candelaria 12, tel: 922 866 112.* Famous for the home-cooking of its owner, Juana de Dios Navarro, this restaurant has a wood-fired oven to grill fresh fish.

LA CALETA

La Caleta €€ *Calle El Meuella 19, tel: 922 780 650.* This great harbourside fish restaurant offers the real flavour of the Tenerife coast. It has all its dishes laid out to view as if in a huge market stall, so you simply choose and point.

LOS ABRIGOS

Restaurante Los Abrigos €€ *Paseo Maritimo, tel: 922 170 261.* Wonderful port-side restaurant with extensive menu of fish, from *abadejo* (pollack) to *vieja* (parrot fish). Crowded at weekend lunchtimes. Closed on Wednesdays, but the next door Perlas de Mar (closed Mondays) has a similarly serious fish menu.

El Tizón €€€ *Calle La Marina 13, tel: 922 170 326.* A pleasantly decorated upmarket restaurant with a variety of dishes, especially from the sea, including anchovies with peppers and salmon with pasta. It has an extensive wine list, and prides itself on good coffee.

LOS CRISTIANOS

Rio 7 €€€ *Carrer Juan Bariajo1, tel: 922 797 636.* A good place to eat fish in Los Cristianos, this modest-sized restaurant near the sea wall specialises in *paellas*.

Rose's Cantina €€ *Urb. Oasis del Sur, tel: 922 751 972.* Tourists enjoy this cheerful touch of Mexico on the island, with staff suitably dressed and refreshing margaritas available at the bar *Enchiladas* and *fajitas* are always on the menu that includes Speedy Gonzalez prawns.

El Sol Transversal *General Franco, s/n, Los Cristianos, tel: 922 790 569.* Classic French cuisine is the speciality of the house in this highly recommended restaurant. Open for dinner only, closed Monday.

PLAYA DE LAS AMÉRICAS

Molino Blanco €€€€ *Avenida Austria 1, tel: 922 796 282.* Charcoal grills and wood-fired ovens are the keynote of this well-known restaurant, which has such delights as suckling pig (*cochinillo*), ostrich (*avastruz*), hare (*ciervo*) and boar (*jabalí*) as well as fresh fish. It has an animated atmosphere in its three dining rooms, with live music, and the landmark white windmill makes it easy to find.

La Rana €€€ *Parque Santaiago IV, tel: 922 752 222.* There's a touch of Gallego cooking in this attractive rural-style restaurant set amid the modern buildings. You can dine indoors or on the terrace, and a barbecue serves up lamb and veal chops. There is lots to choose from on the menu, and many Spanish come here to try it out.

Restaurante a la Carta Poseidón €€€€ *Calle Londres, s/n, Playas del Duque, tel. 922 713 335.* The haute-cuisine restaurant of the Grand Hotel Anthelia Park. Beautifully presented, interesting dishes such as smoked salmon with hand-made goat's cheese, and tender fillets of sole stuffed with extremely tasty small shrimps and spinach.

Restaurante La Tasca €€€ *Gran Hotel Bahia del Duque, Gran Meliá, Calle Alcade Walter Paetzmann, s/n, tel: 746 900.* A Spanish restaurant in décor, style and cuisine, with staff in traditional costume. Familiar and unusual dishes feature on the menu.